Speaking of Childcare

By Peter Vincent and Naoko Nakazato

NAN'UN-DO

このテキストの音声を無料で視聴（ストリーミング）・ダウンロードできます。自習用音声としてご活用ください。
以下のサイトにアクセスしてテキスト番号で検索してください。

https://nanun-do.com　テキスト番号 [511975]

※ 無線 LAN（WiFi）に接続してのご利用を推奨いたします。
※ 音声ダウンロードは Zip ファイルでの提供になります。お使いの機器によっては別途ソフトウェア（アプリケーション）の導入が必要となります。

※ Speaking of Childcare 音声ダウンロードページは以下の QR コードからもご利用になれます。

Speaking of Childcare
保育学生のための英語コミュニケーション

Copyright © 2019
by Peter Vincent and Naoko Nakazato

No part of this book may be reproduced in any form without written permission from the authors and Nan'un-do Co., Ltd.

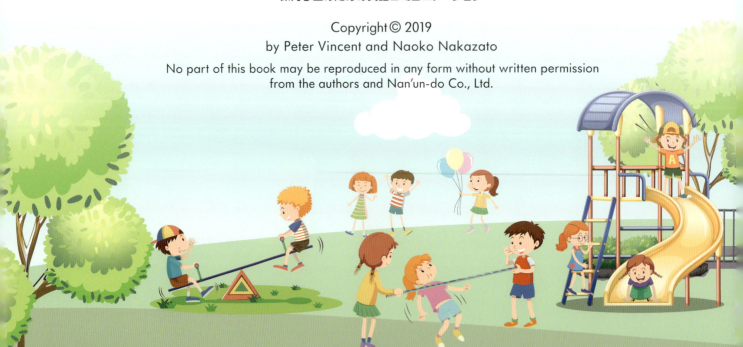

Preface

Welcome to *Speaking of Childcare*, a textbook written for Japanese students who aim to be nursery school or kindergarten teachers. The text is designed for active communication with numerous activities and role plays. The speaking, listening, and writing activities are enhanced with colorful illustrations that make practice situations more concrete as you prepare to communicate with your students and their parents. It includes practice in greeting students and parents in the morning, asking students to perform various tasks, and communicating to parents about student behavior and issues. The text includes a wide variety of vocabulary and expressions, along with a glossary and a variety of vocabulary-review exercises.

To make the most of this textbook, we would like you to remember one thing: Don't be afraid of making mistakes. Making mistakes and learning from them is how you improve your English skills, so please try your best.

We very much enjoyed writing this textbook and hope that you have an equally enjoyable time practicing childcare English.

『Speaking of Childcare』にようこそ。本書は将来保育園や幼稚園の先生を目指している学生のために書かれたもので，多数のアクティビティやロールプレイができるようデザインされています。スピーキング，リスニング，ライティングなどの練習をカラフルなイラストで表現することで，子供や保護者とのコミュニケーション練習をよりわかりやすいアクティビティにしています。朝の挨拶，子供への指示，子供の行動や問題などを保護者に伝える方法など，さまざまな英語表現が含まれており，多数の単語と表現や復習のための様々な練習問題に加え，用語集も付いています。

本書を最も有効に活用していただくためにひとつ覚えておいていただきたいことがあります。間違いを恐れないでください。間違いから学ぶことが英語のスキルを上達させることにつながります。恥ずかしがらず，思い切ってトライしてみてください。

著者一同にとって，本書を書くのは非常に楽しいプロセスでした。みなさんも，本書を使って保育園や幼稚園で使える英語を学ぶことを，楽しいと感じていただけることを願っています。

Peter Vincent and Naoko Nakazato
Seitoku University

CONTENTS

Classroom English 5

Unit 1   What's your name? 6

Unit 2   Where are you from? 12

Unit 3   Good morning! 18

Unit 4   Are you OK? 26

Unit 5   What are you doing? 32

Unit 6   How are you feeling? 38

Unit 7   What's she like? 46

Unit 8   Do's and don'ts 54

Review of Units 1 to 8 63

Unit 9   Let's eat lunch! 68

Unit 10   What do you want to do? 74

Unit 11   What do you have to do? 84

Unit 12   I need to go potty 92

Unit 13   Good job! 100

Unit 14   Injuries and emergencies 108

Unit 15   We're going to go outside 117

Review of Units 9 to 15 123

Appendix 126

Glossary 131

Classroom English

▶ Try to speak as much English as you can in class. Here are some expressions you might need to use:
クラス内ではできるだけ英語で話しましょう。以下の表現を参考にしてください：

1. May I ask a question?　　　　　　　　　　　質問してもいいですか？
2. Could you repeat that, please?　　　　　　すみません，もう一度言っていただけますか？
3. Pardon?　　　　　　　　　　　　　　　　　〃
4. Could you speak more slowly, please?　　もっとゆっくり言っていただけますか？
5. How do you spell _____?　　　　_____ はどのようにつづりますか？
6. Could you write it on the board, please?　それをホワイトボードに書いていただけますか？
7. What does _____ mean?　　　　_____ はどういう意味ですか？
8. How do you say _____ in English?　_____ は英語でどのように言いますか？
9. Could you explain that again, please?　　もう一度説明してください。
10. OK, I understand.　　　　　　　　　　　　はい，わかりました。

▶ And here are some expressions your teacher might say:
先生は以下の表現を使います。

1. Please listen carefully.　　　　　　　　注意して聞いてください。
2. Please repeat.　　　　　　　　　　　　もう一度くりかえしてください。
3. Please answer the question.　　　　　質問に答えてください。
4. Please open your books.　　　　　　　本を開けてください。
5. Please close your books.　　　　　　　本を閉じてください。
6. Please don't look at your books.　　　本を見ないでください。
7. Work in pairs. / Work with a classmate.　ペアになって行ってください。／
　　　　　　　　　　　　　　　　　　　　　クラスメイトと行ってください。
8. Look at page _____.　　　　_____ ページを見てください。
9. Please speak louder.　　　　　　　　　もっと大きな声で言ってください。
10. Do you understand?　　　　　　　　　わかりますか？

Unit 1
What's your name?
お名前は？

Speaking スピーキング

Dialogue 1

Melissa: Hi, I'm Melissa. What's your name?
Risa: Risa.
Melissa: How old are you, Risa?
Risa: Five.
Melissa: I'm five, too! Where do you live?
Risa: Kashiwa.
Melissa: Really? I live in Matsudo.

Dialogue 2

Alice: This is Keiko Akimoto, a new teacher.
Mr. Anderson: Hi Keiko! I'm Robert Anderson, the principal of the school.
Keiko: Hi, Mr. Anderson. Nice to meet you.
Mr. Anderson: Nice to meet you, too. Please call me Rob.
Keiko: OK, Rob. I'm looking forward to* working with you.

* look forward to ～ 〜を楽しみにする

Grammar 1

Questions and Answers
質問と答え

What is (What's) your name?	(My name is) Nao Nakamura.
How do you spell your first name?	N-A-O.
What is your last name again?	It is (It's) Nakamura.
	It's spelled N-A-K-A-M-U-R-A.
How old are you?	(I'm) 26 years old.
Where do you live?	(I live in) Chiba City.
What do you do?	I'm a kindergarten teacher.
What do you (like to) do in your free time?	I play the piano.

Unit 1　What's your name?

Practice 1

▶**Matching**　質問の答えを探そう

Put the correct letters into the spaces to match the questions with the correct answers.
1〜8までの質問に対して最も適切な答えをA〜Hから選んで空欄に記入しましょう。

1. What's your name?　　　　　　　　　　　　_____
2. What do you like to do in your free time?　_____
3. What do you do?　　　　　　　　　　　　　_____
4. How old are you?　　　　　　　　　　　　 _____
5. Where do you live?　　　　　　　　　　　　_____
6. How do you spell your last name?　　　　 _____
7. What's your last name again?　　　　　　 _____
8. How are you?　　　　　　　　　　　　　　_____

A. I'm 18.
B. Great, thanks.
C. It's Yoshida.
D. N-A-K-A-M-U-R-A.
E. I'm a university student.
F. In Mito, Ibaraki prefecture.*
G. Kelly Green.
H. I play tennis every weekend.

*prefecture　県

Grammar 2
Present Tense
現在形

5

be 動詞　　　　　　　　**一般動詞**

I'm a student.　　　　　We play basketball.
You are smart.　　　　　You study English at school.
Lee is tall.　　　　　　　They draw pictures.

Practice 2

▶ **Pair Work** ペアワーク
Take turns making sentences about the following people.
以下の人たちについて説明する文を，パートナーと交代で作りましょう。

> **Example:** He's Brian Porter.
> He's 26 years old.
> He's a kindergarten* teacher.
> He hangs out* with his friends in his free time.

*kindergarten 幼稚園　　hang out 出かける，出歩く

Example
Brian Porter

1. Dana Vance

2. Bin Karanu

3. Nana Takai

26 years old
kindergarten teacher
hangs out with friends

27 years old
nursery school* teacher
does yoga

16 years old
high school student
plays piano

43 years old
school principal
reads and listens to music

4. Jun Takayama

5. Trang Nguyen

6. Anna Belinsky

7. Cheri Jones /
Terri Jones

15 years old
middle school student
plays soccer

5 years old
kindergarten student
plays with his friends

22 years old
princess
dances

8 months old /
8 months old
babies (twins)
always have free time and always play

*nursery school 保育園

Unit 1　What's your name?

> **Note: Present Tense**
> 一般動詞の現在形は，習慣的に行っている動作や現在の事実を表すときに使います。例えば，**I play piano.** は，「私はピアノを弾きます。」と訳されることが多いですが，実際は「私は（ふだん）ピアノを弾きます。」という意味を表します。また，**I have a dog.** は，「私は犬を（現在）飼っています。」という，現在の事実を表しています。

Practice 3

▶**Pair Work**　ペアワーク

Take turns asking and answering questions about the people in **Practice 2**.
Practice 2 の人たちについて，パートナーと交代で質問を作り，それに答えましょう。

Example:　A: What does Brian Porter do?
　　　　　　B: He's a kindergarten teacher.
　　　　　　A: How old is Brian?
　　　　　　B: He's 26 years old.
　　　　　　A: What does Brian do in his free time?
　　　　　　B: He hangs out with friends.

Practice 4

▶**Listening**　リスニング

Listen to the teacher's introduction to new parents and write in the missing words.
先生が初めて会う保護者に自己紹介をしています。次のあいさつ文を聞いて，空欄を埋めましょう。

_____ , everyone. I'm Seiko Numazaki, a _____

_____ here at Sunshine Kindergarten. This is my _____ .

I teach Himawari Gumi. I _____ will be happy at

Sunshine. I want to get to know _____ so I can be a

better teacher for them and _____ .

Our _____ them physically* and mentally* strong.

We also want to teach social skills* so that they can communicate better _____

_____ and adults. I believe _____ that

children show respect* _____ and get along* well.

*physically 身体的に　　mentally 精神的に　　social skills 社会的な技能
show respect 敬意を払う　　get along 仲良くする

Practice 5

▶ **Pair Work** ペアワーク

Complete the questions and then ask your questions to another student. After you have finished, prepare to introduce your partner to the class.

Questions と Answers の枠内にある質問を完成させ，パートナーに質問しましょう。そのあと，パートナーをクラスに紹介しましょう。

> **Example:** What do you study?
> (I study) Childhood education.*
>
> When is your birthday?
> (It's) April 22nd.
>
> What do you like to do in your free time?
> (I like to) Watch TV.

* childhood education 幼児教育

Questions	Answers
1. What ... name?	
2. What ... do?	
3. What ... study?	
4. When ... birthday?	
5. Where ... live?	
6. What ... do ... free time?	

Practice 6

▶**School Supplies** 学用品

Choose the correct name from the box to match the picture. Remember as many words as you can.
絵に合う単語を枠内から選んで書き入れましょう。できるだけ多くの単語を覚えましょう。

Key Words

| apron エプロン　　bath towel バスタオル　　sheet シーツ　　backpack リュックサック, バックパック |
| blanket 毛布　　pillow まくら　　indoor shoes 上履き　　lunchbox お弁当箱　　bib よだれかけ |
| rain boots 長靴　　chopsticks お箸　　toothbrush and toothpaste 歯ブラシと歯磨き粉 |
| swimsuit and swim cap 水着と水泳帽　　Thermos 水筒　　tissues ティッシュ　　underpants 下着のパンツ |

1. _____　2. _____　3. _____　4. _____

5. _____　6. _____　7. _____　8. _____

9. _____　10. _____　11. _____　12. _____

13. _____　14. _____　15. _____　16. _____

Unit 2

Where are you from?

どこから来たの？（出身地は？）

Speaking スピーキング

Dialogue 1

Ms. Ota: Where are you from, Miguel?
Miguel: I'm from the Philippines.
Ms. Ota: Oh, really? I love the Philippines. Where's your hometown?
Miguel: Manila.
Ms. Ota: Oh, Manila is a big city. Do you like living in Japan?
Miguel: It's OK. I miss* my grandparents.
Ms. Ota: Oh, I bet* you do.

Dialogue 2

Misato: Where are you from, Pei?
Pei: I'm from Beijing, China.
Misato: Oh, really? What's Beijing like?
Pei: It's a big city and it's very crowded*, like Tokyo. Do you live in Tokyo?
Misato: No, I don't. I live in Saitama.
Pei: Is it far?
Misato: Not so far. It takes about 30 minutes by train from here.

Dialogue 3

Serina: Where are you from, Awan?
Awan: My dad is from India, but my mom is Japanese. I was born in Japan.
Serina: I want to go to India someday.* Do you speak Japanese?
Awan: Yes, I do.
Serina: That's nice. I speak just a little.

*miss 恋しがる　　I bet ~ それは～に違いない　　crowded 混んでいる　　someday いつか

Grammar

Questions and Answers in Present Tense
現在形の質問と答え

Where are you from?	(I'm from) Canada.
What is your hometown?	(It's) Osaka.
What's Tokyo like?	It's exciting.
Do you speak English?	Yes, but just a little.
Are you Japanese?	No, I'm Korean.

Practice 1

▶ **Fill in the Blanks** 穴埋め問題

Write in the correct form of the verbs in the conversation below.
カッコ内の動詞を最も適切な形にかえて空欄に記入しましょう。

Ms. Yokoyama: Hi, Carla. I _____ (be) Mitsuko Yokoyama, Pedro's kindergarten teacher.

Carla: It _____ (be) nice to _____ (meet) you, Ms. Yokoyama.

Pedro: Nice to _____ (meet) you, Yokoyama Sensei.

Ms. Yokoyama: Please _____ (call) me Mitsuko.

Pedro: OK, Mitsuko.

Ms. Yokoyama: And where _____ (be) you from?

Carla: We _____ (be) from Peru. We _____ (speak) Spanish at home, but Pedro also _____ (speak) English well. He _____ (do) not speak Japanese, though.

Practice 2

▶Nationality and Language 国籍と言語

Student A should look at the chart below. **Student B** should turn to **Appendix 1**. Take turns asking questions and write down the answers in the blanks below, as shown in the example.

Student A は下の表を見て，Student B は Appendix 1 を開いてください。交代で質問をし，空欄に正しい国名，国籍，言語を入れましょう。

Example:
Student A: Where's Yelena from?
Student B: She's from Russia.
Student A: How do you spell "Russia"?
Student B: "R-U-S-S-I-A." What's her nationality?*
Student A: She's Russian. What language does she speak?
Student B: She speaks Russian.

*nationality 国籍

Student A

	Name	Country	Nationality	Language
1.	Yelena (she)	Russia	Russian	Russian
2.	Charlotte (she)	_____	British	_____
3.	Min-jun (he)	_____	_____	Korean
4.	Mai (she)	Vietnam	Vietnamese	_____
5.	Somchai (he)	_____	Thai	Thai
6.	Adam (he)	The United States of America	_____	_____
7.	Yun (she)	_____	Chinese	_____
8.	Miguel (he)	Brazil	_____	Portuguese

Practice 3

▶Listening リスニング

Listen to the passage and write in the missing words below. 英文を聞いて，空欄を埋めましょう。

Kim comes from _____. Her _____ is a computer engineer.
Her mother is _____, but she works part-time, too. Kim is
_____ and is _____.
She _____, but she doesn't like math.* _____
_____ the most. She wants to be an artist _____.
She speaks Korean _____, but all her friends _____.
Her Japanese is perfect.

*math 算数

Unit 2 **Where are you from?**

Practice 4

▶**Pair Work** ペアワーク

Practice the following conversation using the substitute words below each picture.
それぞれの絵の情報を，以下の会話にあてはめてみましょう。

> **Example:** Ms. Kimura: Reiko, this is <u>Somsak</u>. He comes from <u>Thailand</u>.
> Reiko: Hi, <u>Somsak</u>. Do you want to <u>play soccer</u> with me?
> Somsak: Sure. (That) Sounds* <u>great</u>!
> Reiko: Let's go!

* sounds ~ 〜に聞こえる，〜だね（Sounds good! よさそうだね！ いいね！）

1. Liam
   He/Canada
   play soccer
   nice

2. Sophia
   She/Brazil
   play in the playground*
   fun

3. Yun
   She/China
   read
   nice

4. Habib
   He/Kenya
   play catch*
   terrific*

5. Min-jun
   She/South Korea
   play tag*
   like fun

6. Sergei
   He/Russia
   play hide-and-seek*
   good

* playground 園庭，校庭　　play catch キャッチボールをする　　terrific すばらしい　　tag 鬼ごっこ
hide-and-seek (play hide-and-seek) かくれんぼ（かくれんぼをする）

Practice 5

▶ Find Someone Who こんな人いるかな？

Complete the questions on the left of the chart below. Then find someone who answers "yes" to the questions and write their names on the right. Try to talk to as many people as you can.

表の左側の質問文を完成させ，その質問に "Yes" と答えられる人を見つけたら，その人の名前を右側の欄に記入してください。できるだけ多くの人に質問しましょう。

Example: A: Do you have a foreign* friend?
B: Yes, I do.

* foreign 外国の

Find someone who …	Names
1. … likes sports. Question: _____	
2. … listens to music every day. Question: _____	
3. … wants to go to America. Question: _____	
4. … speaks a little English. Question: _____	
5. … is from Tokyo. Question: _____	
6. … has a foreign friend. Question: _____	
7. … wants to teach kindergarten. Question: _____	
8. … plays tennis. Question: _____	
9. … sometimes sleeps in class. Question: _____	

Unit 2　Where are you from?

Culture Note

The words for various sounds are different in each language. Japanese has many such words, but English has fewer and they are often used as verbs.

音の表し方は国や文化によって異なります。日本には擬音語や擬態語がたくさんありますが、英語では音を表す言葉はあまり多くありません。また それらは、しばしば動詞として使われます。

Practice 6

▶ **Sounds**　いろいろな音（擬音）

Practice making the following sounds.　英語でいろいろな音を練習してみましょう。　13

honk honk / beep beep
車のクラクションの音
［ブーブー］

pop
風船などが割れる音
［パーン］

crash
壊れる音
［ガシャン］

thud
重いものが落ちる音
［ドスン］

snap
棒などが折れる音
［ポキン、パキン］

crunch crunch
食べるときの
カリカリ音

bang
ドアなどを強くたたく音
［ドン、バン］

boom
［ドカーン］

rip
破れる音
［ビリッ］

splash
水がはねる音
［ピシャッ］

ring ring
電話の音
［リンリン］

boo hoo 人の泣き声
［ウェーンウェーン、
シクシク、メソメソ］

achoo
くしゃみ
［ハクション］

ruff ruff
犬の鳴き声
［ワンワン］

squeak squeak
ネズミの鳴き声
［チューチュー］

moo
牛の鳴き声
［モー］

oink oink
ブタの鳴き声
［ブーブー］

meow
ネコの鳴き声
［ニャー］

tweet tweet
鳥の鳴き声
［ピーピー］

cock a doodle do
ニワトリの鳴き声
［コケコッコー］

Now act out the sounds above without making any sound.
音を出さずに上記の音（擬音）を表現してみましょう。

Unit 3
Good morning!
おはよう!

Speaking　スピーキング

Dialogue 1

Ms. Suzuki: Good morning! You're early today.
Steven: Yeah, I want to play with Michael.
Ms. Suzuki: Oh, that sounds fun. Michael is playing in the classroom.

Dialogue 2

Ms. Kubota: Good morning! Oh, you're with your daddy today!
Jun: Yeah, it's Monday.
Ms. Kubota: That's right. You come to school with your dad every Monday.
Jun: Yes. And he picks me up* on Tuesday and Thursday, too.

Dialogue 3

Ms. Kimura: What's the matter*, Ken? Why are you crying?
Mr. Masui (father): He's crying because we're late.
Ms. Kimura: You're fine, Ken. It's no problem. Come into the classroom.

*　pick up　迎えに行く（来る）　　What's the matter?　どうしたの？

Grammar 1
Two-Word Verbs
二語動詞

With many two-word verbs such as "pick up," the pronoun cannot be at the end, but must be in the middle of the two-word verb.

pick 人 up / pick up 人＝人を迎えに行く，来る

※迎えに行く相手（取りにいく物）が目的格の代名詞である場合（her, him, it など）は，pick 人／物 up。それ以外の名詞（John, my mother など）なら pick up のあとでも pick と up の間でもどちらでも可。

パパがいつもぼくをお迎えに来るの。

Correct
○ My dad always picks me up.
○ John's dad always picks John up.
○ John's dad always picks up John.

Incorrect
× My dad always picks up me.

Unit 3   Good morning!

Textbook English vs. Real English

Textbook English	Real English
A: Hello! How are you? B: I'm fine, thank you, and you? A: I'm fine, thank you.	A: Hi, how are you? B: Great! How are you? A: I'm good. / Fine. / OK. B: Good!

18

More "Real" English

Children do not necessarily greet other people like adults. They are much more spontaneous and unpredictable. Read the following conversation and practice with your partner.
大人同士のあいさつと子供相手のあいさつには違いがあります。子供は "How are you?" と言われても，大人に "How are you?" と返すとはかぎりません。まったく別の話題について話し始めるかもしれません！

Ms. Jones: Hi Kate! How are you?
Kate: Good. Ms. Jones, I just got a hamster!
Ms. Jones: Oh, wow!* A hamster? That's great! Is it a boy or girl?
Kate: It's a girl. Her name is Lilly.

* wow! ワーッ！

Practice 1

▶ **Listening**   リスニング   19

Listen to the conversation and write in the missing words below.
会話を聞いて空欄を埋めましょう。

Ms. Mathers: Good morning Yuka. _____?
Yuka: Not so good.
Ms. Mathers: Really? _____?
Yuka: I _____ stomachache.*
Ms. Ota: She _____ any appetite.*
Ms. Mathers: _____.

* stomachache 腹痛   appetite 食欲

19

Grammar 2
Present and Present Continuous Tenses
現在形と現在進行形

Past　　present　　Future
過去　　現在　　　未来

Use present tense for activities you do regularly. Use the present continuous to talk about activities you are doing at the present moment.
一般動詞の現在形は，普段習慣的に行っている行動を表すときに使います。現在進行形はその一時だけ行っている行動を表すときに使います。

Present tense:
一般動詞の現在形

I brush my teeth twice a day.
He goes to school on weekdays.
I usually wake up at 7 a.m.

Present continuous tense:
現在進行形
（be 動詞＋ ~ing）

They are watching TV right now.
I am eating dinner.
Mika's playing in her room.

* brush (one's teeth)（～の歯を）磨く

Practice 2

▶ **Verb Practice**　動詞の使い分け

Choose the correct answer. Consider whether the speakers are talking about a regular activity or an activity being done at the present time.
カッコ内の2つの選択肢のうち，正しいものを丸で囲みましょう。話し手が日常的に行っている行動について語っているのか，一時的に行っている行動なのかに注意しましょう。

1. A: Mari (is doing / does) homework now.
   B: Wow! That's great! She usually (is waiting / waits) to do homework until late.

2. (Does / Is) it windy outside?

3. We (don't read / aren't reading) newspapers, but we read news on the internet.

4. I don't want to eat now. I (still play / am still playing) video games.

5. A: Where is Ken?
   B: He (watches / is watching) TV in the living room now. Don't you remember? He (watches / is watching) cartoons every Sunday.

* homework 宿題　　until ～まで　　still まだ　　cartoons マンガ

Unit 3　**Good morning!**

Practice 3

▶**What Are You Doing?**　今何してるの？

Work in pairs. Ask your partner what the characters in each picture are doing. Take turns asking and answering questions. Use the subject shown under the picture.

パートナーと交代で，子供たちがそれぞれ今何をしているのかを英語で言ってみましょう。
絵の下の名前を使って質問してください。

Example: A: What's Rick doing?
B: He's washing his hands.

Rick

1. Erika

2. Risa

3. Shiori and Adam

4. Fabio

5. Sergei

6. Mia

7. Ben, Emma, and Jack

8. Sofia

Practice 4

▶**Nursery School Teacher Activities** 先生は毎日何するの？

What do nursery school teachers do every day? Choose the right words from the box to make sentences. Do not forget to put "s" for subjects that are third-person singular.

保育園の先生は毎日どんなことをしていますか？ 枠内から動詞を選んで文を完成させましょう。主語が三人称単数の場合は動詞に"s"がつきます。

| prepare*   write   read   play   take   show   sing |

1. She _____ games with children.

2. He _____ songs with children.

3. They _____ lunch for children.

4. She _____ children out for walks.

5. They _____ stories to children.

6. He _____ children how to make *origami*.

7. She _____ messages to parents.

*prepare 準備をする

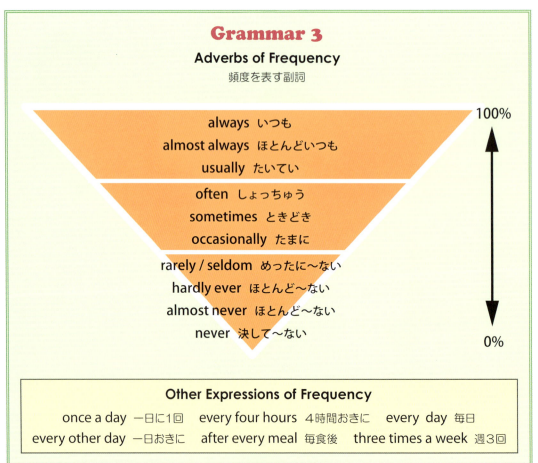

Unit 3　Good morning!

Textbook English vs. Real English

Real English: Let's give short, simple answers!
短くシンプルに答えてみよう！

In answering questions, English textbook dialogues often teach something like:
英語のテキストには，質問に対してよく次のような答え方がのっています。

　Question: How often do you brush your teeth?
　Answer: I brush my teeth twice a day.

Of course, it is useful to know how to make complete sentences, but in real life, we often give short answers, just as Japanese do in their own language.
もちろん，完璧な文を覚えておくのは大事ですが，実際には日本人もよく使うように，短く答えることが多いのです。

　Question: How often do you brush your teeth?
　Answer: Twice a day.

Practice 5

▶**Short Answers**　短く答えてみよう

Write short answers that are true for you.　自分のことについて短く答えてみましょう。

Example: How often do you brush your teeth?
　　　　　　Usually twice a day.

Question　　　　　　　　　　　　　　　Your short answer

1. How often do you brush your teeth?　_____
2. How often do you take a bath/shower?*　_____
3. How often do you drink water?　_____
4. How often do you do your homework?　_____
5. How often do you get at least* 8 hours of sleep?　_____
6. How often do you get a cold?　_____
7. How often do you eat dessert?　_____

*take a shower　シャワーをあびる　　at least　少なくとも

Practice 6

▶**Pair Work**　ペアワーク

Ask the questions from **Practice 5** to a partner.　Practice 5 を見てパートナーに質問しましょう。

Practice 7

▶ Find Someone Who   こんな人いるかな？

First, complete the questions on the left of the chart below. Then find someone who answers "yes" to the question and write their name on the right. Try to talk to as many people as you can.

表の左側の質問文を完成させ，その質問に "Yes" と答えられる人を見つけたら，その人の名前を右側の欄に記入してください。できるだけ多くの人に質問しましょう。

> **Example:** Question: How often do you exercise?*
> Answer: Usually every day.

* exercise 運動（する）

Find someone who …	Names
1.　… usually brushes their teeth three times a day. Question: _____	
2.　… gets a medical check-up* once a year or more. Question: _____	
3.　… usually eats dessert after dinner. Question: _____	
4.　… always takes a train or bus to school. Question: _____	
5.　… rarely goes to a doctor. Question: _____	
6.　… takes a shower at least five times a week. Question: _____	
7.　… usually exercises every day. Question: _____	
8.　… rarely or never gets a cold. Question: _____	

* check-up (medical check-up) 健康診断

Unit 3　Good morning!

Practice 8

▶**Skit**　スキット

Make a conversation about a teacher greeting a child and her/his parents coming to school in the morning. Please feel free to make your skit* creative and interesting!
朝，先生が子供や保護者にあいさつをするシーンを思い浮かべて会話を作ってみましょう。想像力を使ってできるだけ楽しいスキットにしましょう！

＊skit　スキット，寸劇，短い演劇

Unit 4

Are you OK?
大丈夫？

Speaking スピーキング

Dialogue 1

Ms. Suzue: Hi, Steven! Are you all right? You don't look so good.
Steven: Waaa!
Ms. Meadows (mother): He has a cold.
Ms. Suzue: Oh, that's too bad. Does he have a fever*?
Ms. Meadows: No, he feels a little tired, though. He wants to wear his mask today. Is that OK?
Ms. Suzue: Yes, it's fine. We'll take good care* of him.

Dialogue 2

Ms. Imura: Are you OK, Markie?
Markie: I have a stomachache. It hurts.*
Ms. Imura: This is medicine* for your stomach. Drink this and you'll feel better.*
Markie: Okay. Yuck!* This tastes* bad.

Dialogue 3

Ms. Tamura: Good morning, Maria. Why are you crying?
Ms. Gomez: Maria doesn't want to come to school today.
Ms. Tamura: Oh? Why is that?
Ms. Gomez: Because she had a headache* last night. She's better now.
Ms. Tamura: Well, don't worry, Maria. Just relax until you feel OK.

*fever 熱　take care (take good care) 世話をする　hurt 痛む，痛める　medicine 薬
feel better 気分がよくなる　Yuck! ゲーッ！　taste 味がする，味わう　headache 頭痛

Unit 4　Are you OK?

Key Words: Symptoms (症状)

Sickness　病気

fever 熱　　influenza (the flu) インフルエンザ
vomit (vomiting) 吐く　　sweat (sweaty) 汗(汗まみれの)

Colds　風邪

sneeze (sneezing) くしゃみ（をする）
sore throat のどの痛み　　cough (coughing) 咳（をする）
headache 頭痛

Other　その他

stomachache 腹痛　　nosebleed 鼻血　　rash 湿疹
toothache 歯痛　　itchy かゆい　　backache 腰痛
pain 痛み

Practice 1

▶ **Listening**　リスニング

Listen to the CD and circle the letter of the medical condition that is being described.
CDを聞いて，どんな症状について説明されているかを選びましょう。

1. a) A stomachache　b) A high fever　c) A cough　d) A backache
2. a) A cough　b) Vomiting　c) A sneeze　d) A sore throat
3. a) A headache　b) A backache　c) A sore throat　d) A stomachache
4. a) A toothache　b) A backache　c) A stomachache　d) Vomiting
5. a) Sweating　b) A fever　c) A sore throat　d) A stomachache
6. a) Influenza　b) A rash　c) Itchy　d) A toothache
7. a) A nosebleed　b) Sweaty　c) Itchy　d) A rash

＊dentist 歯医者　　skin 肌

Practice 2

▶ **Symptoms** 症状を説明しよう

Put the correct word from the box in the sentences below.
枠内からあてはまる単語を選び，空欄に記入しましょう。

| toothache 歯痛　　itchy かゆい　　fever 熱　　dizzy めまいがする |
| stomachache 胃痛, 腹痛　　headache 頭痛　　cough 咳　　cold 風邪 |

1. I have a _____ .

2. My son has a _____ .

3. I have a bad _____ .

4. I have a _____ .

5. I need to go to the dentist because

   I have a _____ .

6. I'm _____ .

7. I have a _____ .

8. I'm _____ .

Practice 3

▶ **Verbs**   病状を表す動詞

Put the correct verb from the box in the sentences below. Use the correct verb tense.
正しい動詞を枠内から選び，空欄に記入しましょう。必要なら動詞を適切な形にかえてみましょう。

have (use three times)   be (use three times)   hurt

1. I _____ sick.

   I think I _____ the flu.

2. I have an allergy.

   I _____ itchy.

3. Satsuki _____ a cough.

4. I _____ a toothache.

   My tooth _____ .

5. I _____ dizzy.

Practice 4

▶Medical Products 医療品

Write the correct word from the box below under the picture it describes.
絵に合う単語を枠内から選んで絵の下に書き入れましょう。

Key Words

Medical Products（医療品）

ambulance 救急車　　Band-Aid バンドエイド　　bandages 包帯　　cast ギプス　　cotton swabs 綿棒
cough syrup 咳止めシロップ　　crutches 松葉づえ　　eye drops 目薬　　ice pack アイスパック
health insurance card 保険証　　nurse and patient 看護師と患者　　ointment 塗り薬　　pills 薬
scale 体重計　　shot 注射　　thermometer 体温計　　tweezers ピンセット　　wheelchair 車いす

 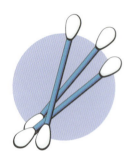  

1. _____ 2. _____ 3. _____ 4. _____

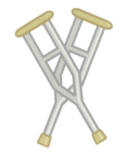   

5. _____ 6. _____ 7. _____ 8. _____

9. _____ 10. _____ 11. _____ 12. _____

13. _____ 14. _____ 15. _____ 16. _____

17. _____ 18. _____

Practice 5

▶**Listening** リスニング 29

Listen to the conversation and write in the missing words below. 会話を聞いて空欄を埋めましょう。

Dr. Jones: What's the matter, Kenta?

Kenta: I don't _____ . I want to _____ .

Dr. Jones: Your forehead _____ . Let me check and see if you _____ .

Kenta: My head _____ .

Dr. Jones: Oh, you _____ . That's too bad. Go over there and _____ . Your parents will _____ soon.

Practice 6

▶**Skit** スキット

Make a conversation between a teacher and a student who is not feeling well. Be prepared to perform your skit in front of the class.
先生と具合の悪い生徒との会話を作って，クラスの前で発表しましょう。

Unit 5
What are you doing?
何してるの？

Speaking スピーキング

Dialogue 1

   Yasu: Can I read this book?
Mr. Kerry: Sure, Yasu. Everyone's reading now.
   Yasu: I want this one, too.
Mr. Kerry: No, take just one. Then go back* to your seat.

Dialogue 2

Ms. Nakamura: Don't forget to wash your hands.
    Brad: OK. I'm washing them.
Ms. Nakamura: Now turn off* the faucet.*
    Brad: OK.
Ms. Nakamura: Don't wipe* your hands on your clothes. Use the paper towels.*

Dialogue 3

Ms. Kent: It's time to go inside.
Haruki: No, I'm still playing.
Ms. Kent: Sorry, Haruki, but another class is coming now. You can play again later.
Haruki: My hands are dirty.*
Ms. Kent: Look. Everyone is washing their hands in the sink.* Be sure to use soap and water.

*go back 戻る turn off 閉める faucet 蛇口 wipe 拭く
paper towels キッチンペーパー，ペーパータオル
dirty 汚れた sink シンク，流し

Unit 5 **What are you doing?**

Grammar
Special Verbs
特殊な動詞

Some verbs, like the "be" verb, are usually not put in the present continuous tense. Other verbs normally not used in the present continuous include "love," "need," "want," and "know."

動詞の中には，be 動詞や "love", "need", "want", "know" のように，現在進行形にできない動詞があります。

Example: ○ I need a pen now.　　× I'm needing a pen now.
　　　　　　 ○ I know him.　　　　× I'm knowing him.

Practice 1

▶**Fill in the Blanks**　穴埋め問題

Complete the conversations with the correct form of the verb.
カッコ内の動詞を適切な形にして空欄を埋め，会話を完成させましょう。

Mr. Tanaka: It _____ (be) naptime,* Shinsuke. Everyone _____ (change) into* their pajamas.

Shinsuke: I _____ (be) not sleepy.

Mr. Tanaka: Everyone _____ (get) ready* now.

Sasha: I _____ (need) to go to the toilet.

Mr. Tanaka: OK. Hurry up and come back.

(Later)

Sasha: I _____ (be) back!

Mr. Tanaka: OK, but be quiet. Everyone _____ (take) a nap* now. Lie down and close your eyes.

(Later)

Mr. Tanaka: It _____ (be) time to wake up!

Dana: I _____ (be) sleepy. I _____ (do not) want to get up.

Mr. Tanaka: I _____ (know) how you feel, but everyone _____ (get) up. Look, everyone _____ (get) dressed* now.

Dana: Where _____ (be) my pants? Waa!

Mr. Tanaka: Don't cry. They _____ (be) over there.

*naptime　お昼寝の時間　　change into (your pajamas)　（パジャマに）着替える
get ready　準備する　　nap (take a nap)　昼寝（をする）　　get dressed　着替える

Practice 2

▶**What Are the Children Doing?** 子供たち何してる？

Complete the sentences with the correct verb from the box. Use the present continuous tense.
枠内の動詞から最も適切なものを選び，空欄を埋めてください。現在進行形を使いましょう。

| play (use 3 times) | ~~sleep~~ | jump | swing | slide | read | run |

Example: The children <u>are sleeping</u>.

1. Dewi _____ on a swing.*

2. Mina _____ with a jump rope.*

3. Lisa _____ with a doll.

34

Unit 5   **What are you doing?**

4. Brad _____ .

5. Jason _____ a book.

6. Nana and Shawn _____ catch.

7. Erica and Ben _____ down a slide.*

8. Thanh _____ in the sandbox.*

*swing ブランコ   jump rope なわとび   slide すべり台   sandbox 砂場

Practice 3

▶ **Pair Work**　ペアワーク

Student A should look at the picture below. **Student B** should turn to **Appendix 2**. Tell your partner what the eight children are doing. Find six differences and circle those pictures.

Student A は以下の絵を，Student B は Appendix 2 の絵を見てください。8 人の子供たちが何をしているかをパートナーに説明し，お互いの見ている絵に 6 つの違いを見つけてその絵を丸で囲みましょう。

Student A

＊ jungle gym　ジャングルジム　　monkey bars　うんてい

Unit 5 **What are you doing?**

Practice 4

▶**Writing** ライティング

Write nine sentences about what the people are doing in the picture below.
以下の絵を見て，子供たちがしていることを説明する文を書きましょう。

1. Ms. Kitamura
2. Risa
3. Andy

4. Ken
5. Makoto
6. Harumi

7. Saki and Eric
8. Leo and Mari
9. Mayu

＊serve 食事や飲み物を出す

1. _____
2. _____
3. _____
4. _____
5. _____
6. _____
7. _____
8. _____
9. _____

Unit 6
How are you feeling?
どんな気分？

Speaking スピーキング

Dialogue 1

Ms. Hashimoto: Is everything OK, Eri? You don't look very happy.
Eri: Well, I'm upset* because Keiko is so mean* to me.
Ms. Hashimoto: Keiko, you're not mean to Eri, are you?
Keiko: No, I'm not. But I'm a bit* frustrated* because Eri is so slow.
Ms. Hashimoto: Well, you have to be more patient.* This is her first time to play this game.

Dialogue 2

Ms. Hashimoto: Why are you crying, Jun?
Jun: Seina hit me. She's a bully.*
Ms. Hashimoto: Seina, what's going on?
Seina: I didn't do anything.
Jun: She's lying.* I'm scared of her.
Ms. Hashimoto: You have to be brave,* Jun. And Seina, you have to be nice to others.

*upset 怒っている　　mean いじわるな　　a bit 少し　　frustrated イライラしている　　patient 我慢強い
bully いじめっこ　　lie (lying) うそをつく（ついている）　　be scared of ~ ～が怖い　　brave 勇気がある

Unit 6 How are you feeling?

Key Words

Express your feelings with "~ed" and "~ing" adjectives
~ed や ~ing を使った形容詞で気分を表す

When we talk about feelings, we often use past participles verbs with "ed," such as "I was surprised." We use the "ed" ending when the feeling is inside us. When we talk about some outside event that gives us a feeling, we often use an "ing" ending, such as "The concert was exciting."

"I was surprised." のように主語が人で，その人の感じたことを表すときは，動詞の過去分詞 "~ed" 形を使います。"The concert was exciting." のように，状況やものが自分たちにある感情を起こさせるときは，動詞の "~ing" 形を使います。

It is ~ing. The movie was ~ing. The meeting was ~ing.
interesting おもしろい　　shocking ショッキングな　　exciting わくわくする　　boring つまらない
disappointing がっかりする　　embarrassing 恥ずかしい　　surprising 驚くべき
frustrating イライラする　　confusing 混乱する　　moving 感動する　　relaxing リラックスする

I am ~ed, He/She is ~ed, My brother is ~ed.
interested, shocked, excited, bored, disappointed, embarrassed, surprised, frustrated, confused, moved, relaxed

Practice 1

▶**Feeling Words**　どう感じているの？

Put the words from the box under the correct picture.
絵に合う単語を枠内から選んで書き入れましょう。

Key Words

jealous うらやましがる　　frustrated 欲求不満，イライラする　　embarrassed 恥ずかしがる bored たいくつな　　confused 混乱した　　ashamed 恥じる　　proud 誇りに思う　　excited わくわくする relieved 安心した　　shocked ショックな　　relaxed リラックスした　　angry 怒っている

1. _____ 2. _____ 3. _____ 4. _____

5. _____ 6. _____ 7. _____ 8. _____

9. _____ 10. _____ 11. _____ 12. _____

★ **The difference between "ashamed" and "embarrassed"**

　"Ashamed" means having a feeling of guilt.
　"Embarrassed" means having an emotional feeling of discomfort in front of other people.

★ **Ashamed と embarrassed の違い**

　Ashamed：社会的通念や道徳的に悪いことをしたときや自分に罪の意識を感じる。
　Embarrassed：他人に対して恥ずかしいと感じたとき。人前で恥をかいたとき。

Unit 6　**How are you feeling?**

Practice 2

▶**Feeling Words**　どう感じているの？

Complete the following sentences with the correct words from the box.
枠内から感情を表す最も適切な単語を選び，文を完成させましょう。

excited　irritating イライラする　~~disappointing~~　bored
exciting　~~disappointed~~　confused　boring　scary 怖い
irritated イライラして　confusing　scared 怖がる

Example: My grade is <u>disappointing</u>, so I'm <u>disappointed</u>.

1. I'm _____ because the movie is very _____ .

2. My math* homework* is _____ .
   I'm _____ .

3. My brother is so _____ !
   I'm _____ .

4. The concert is _____ .
   The audience* is _____ .

5. I'm _____ because this book is _____ .

*math 算数　homework 宿題　audience 観客

41

Grammar
Answering Negative Questions
否定の質問文の答え方

In Japanese, the answer to "yes" and "no" questions changes according to whether a question is positive or negative. The answers don't change in English.

日本語と英語では "Yes" や "No" の答え方が異なるときがあるので注意しましょう。

In English, if you are not happy, the answer is always "No." If you are happy, the answer is always "Yes."

英語では，幸せなら答えは常に "Yes"。幸せでなければ答えは常に "No"。

English:	Aren't you happy?	Yes (I'm happy). ♥
		No (I'm not happy). 💔
Japanese:	幸せじゃないの？	うん（幸せじゃない）。💔
		ううん（幸せだよ）。♥
English:	You're happy, aren't you?	Yes (I'm happy). ♥
		No (I'm not happy). 💔
Japanese:	幸せなんだよね？	うん（幸せ）。♥
		ううん（幸せじゃない）。💔

Practice 3

▶**Writing**　ライティング

Look at the pictures and answer the following questions.
絵を見て以下の質問に答えましょう。

Example: The children are happy, aren't they?
Answer: <u>Yes, they are</u>.

1. Isn't she shocked?

   Answer: _____ .

42

Unit 6 How are you feeling?

2. Is he nervous?*

   Answer: _____ .

3. The grade is disappointing, isn't it?

   Answer: _____ .

4. Isn't the class interesting?

   Answer: _____ .

* nervous 緊張した

Practice 4

▶**Mime Activity**　ジェスチャーゲーム

The teacher will give some feeling words to each group. Take turns acting out the words. The other members try to guess what that feeling word is.

先生が各グループに感情を表す単語を書いた紙を渡し，グループの一人がジェスチャーでその単語の意味を表します。ほかのメンバーはその言葉をあててみましょう。

Example:	A: (Use gestures or expressions on your face to describe your feeling.)
	B: Are you sad?
	A: No, I'm not sad.
	C: Are you angry?
	A: Yes, I'm angry! (Finished)

Practice 5

▶Fill in the Blanks 穴埋め問題

Choose the feeling words from the box and fill in the blanks.
枠内から最も適切な単語を選んで文を完成させましょう。

| shocked | disappointed | proud | jealous |
| excited | ashamed | bored | confused |

I'm very good at math. Class is sometimes so easy for me that I get _____ . I got my test back this morning. I thought I did well, so I was _____ and hoped to see a 100 score on it. I was sure I passed* it, but I didn't, so I was _____ to see my low score. I saw that I answered some questions wrong because I was _____ by the directions* on the test. My best friend is not as smart* as me, but she passed it, so I was _____ of her. I told my mother I passed the test, but I was _____ for telling her a lie. Later, I told her the truth*. She said, "telling lies is bad, so I'm _____ in you." Next time, I will study harder* and make my mother _____ of me.

*pass 合格する　directions 指示　smart 賢い　truth 真実　hard 一生懸命に

Unit 6   **How are you feeling?**

Practice 6

▶**Pair Work**   ペアワーク

Imagine how you would feel in the following situations. Describe what your feelings would be in each case.
こんなときどう感じますか？ それぞれの場面で自分がどう感じるかを説明してみましょう。

> **Example:** A strange man talked to you on the street at night.
> ➡ I would be scared*!
>
>   *would（～だったら）～だろう

1. You wake up late and walk into class 30 minutes late.
2. You hear that your friend is going to France this summer.
3. This is your first day of school. You are meeting new classmates and new teachers.
4. You paint* a beautiful picture in class. Everyone loves it.
5. You lose your wallet.* Next day you find it.

                                               *paint 絵を描く   wallet さいふ

Unit 7
What's she like?
彼女はどんな人？

Speaking スピーキング

Dialogue 1 39

Ms. Suzuki: My son is very shy.* Does he talk in class?
Ms. Kerry: Yes, he talks a lot. He's very friendly with everyone.
Ms. Suzuki: Really? I'm relieved* to hear that. Does he study well?
Ms. Kerry: Yes. He's usually a very serious* student, but he's sometimes too active* in class. I often have to tell him to sit down.

Dialogue 2 40

Mr. Black: Robert loves your class, Ms. Kerry. He thinks you're cheerful* and sweet.*
Ms. Kerry: Thank you. That's very kind of you. Your son is very smart, Mr. Black.
Mr. Black: That's good to hear, but he's sometimes a little bossy* when he plays with his younger brothers. What's he like at school?
Ms. Kerry: I don't think he's so bossy, but he sometimes gets silly* and goofy.* He likes to make the other children laugh.*

*shy 恥ずかしがりや　relieved 安心した　serious まじめな　active 活動的な
cheerful 明るい　sweet 優しい　bossy いばっている　silly バカな，ふざけた
goofy ふざけた，お茶目な　laugh 笑う

Note: What does "like" mean?
"Like" の意味は？

"Like" has two common meanings. Students often assume that like means "suki" (好き), but when the "be" verb comes before "like," it means "~ no youna" (〜のような).
"Like" にはおもに2つの意味があります。普段は「好き」という意味にとらえると思いますが，be動詞が前に来ると，「〜のような」という意味になります。

What's he like?　　　彼はどんな人？
What does he like?　彼は何が好き？

Unit 7   What's she like?

Practice 1

▶ **Words to Describe People**   人について説明しよう

Choose the correct word from the box to describe the personality of the people in the pictures.
絵を見てその人たちの性格や特徴を表す最も適切な単語を枠内から選びましょう。

Key Words

| silly/goofy ふざけた，お茶目な   picky 好き嫌いがある   brave 勇気がある   smart 賢い |
| naughty いたずらな   kind/sweet 優しい   honest 正直な   talented 才能がある |
| cheerful 明るい   generous 気前がよい，寛大な   bossy いばった   rude 失礼な |

1. _____   2. _____   3. _____   4. _____

5. _____   6. _____   7. _____   8. _____

9. _____   10. _____   11. _____   12. _____

Practice 2

▶ **More Words to Describe People** 人について説明しよう

Choose the feeling words from the box and fill in the blanks.
枠内から最も適切な単語を選んで文を完成させましょう。

| generous   bossy   rude   picky   talented   naughty   honest   goofy |

1. The teenager sitting in the priority seat* did not move when an elderly* man came into the train. He's _____ .
2. My mother often gives money to poor* people. She's very _____ .
3. Richard always tells the truth.* He's very _____ .
4. Kana always tells other children what to do. She's _____ .
5. Lee likes to make other people laugh by dancing and making silly faces. He's _____ .
6. Dana steals* things and hits other children. She's often _____ .
7. Ami can play the violin very well. She's _____ .
8. There are many kinds* of food that Tatsu hates. He's a _____ eater.

*priority seat 優先席   elderly 高齢者   poor まずしい   truth 真実   steal 盗む   kind 種類

Unit 7　What's she like?

Practice 3

▶ **Writing**　ライティング

Mess and *messy* are useful words!　"mess"と"messy"はとても役に立つ表現です！

| mess: ゴチャゴチャした，面倒な状況（名）　　messy: ゴチャゴチャした，面倒な（形）　　mess up: ゴチャゴチャにする（動） |

What a *mess*!　　　　　　She has *messy* hair.　　It's a *messy* situation.　　You *messed up* my
What a *messy* room!　　　　　　　　　　　　　　　　　　　　　　　　　　　sandcastle!!
The room is *messy*.

Now write sentences to describe the pictures.　絵の状況を表す文を作りましょう。

1. (Teacher to students)

   What _____ !

2. He _____ .

3. (Mother to children)

   Oh, no! You _____ !

Practice 4

▶ **Matching**   状況と絵を合わせよう

Match the communication expressed in the pictures by putting the correct letter after each of the sentences below.

1〜17の文の状況を表している絵をA〜Qから選び，空欄に記入しましょう。

Unit 7 What's she like?

M   N   O   P

Q

1. Do you want to fight? _____
2. I'm in a hurry!* _____
3. I'm really upset! _____
4. I'm tired. _____
5. Stop! _____
6. You're my friend. _____
7. I don't feel so good. _____
8. It stinks.* _____
9. I'm bored. _____

10. I love you. _____
11. I'm confused. _____
12. I'm afraid.* _____
13. I'm relieved. _____
14. I'm sad. _____
15. Yay!* _____
16. Oh, no! You made a mess. _____
17. It's hot. _____

* in a hurry 急いでいる   stink 臭いにおいがする   afraid 怖がる   yay! イェイ！

51

Practice 5

▶ **Family Tree**　家系図を書いてみよう

Part 1: Look at Kevin's family tree below and fill in the blanks using the correct words from the box.
枠内の言葉を使ってケヴィン家の家系図の空欄を埋めましょう。

Key Words 42

sister 姉, 妹	brother 兄, 弟	wife 妻	cousin いとこ	son 息子	father 父
nephew 甥	husband 夫	uncle おじ	granddaughter 孫娘	aunt おば
grandmother 祖母	mother 母	niece 姪	grandfather 祖父	daughter 娘
grandson 孫息子	brother-in-law 義理の兄（弟）	mother-in-law 義理の母

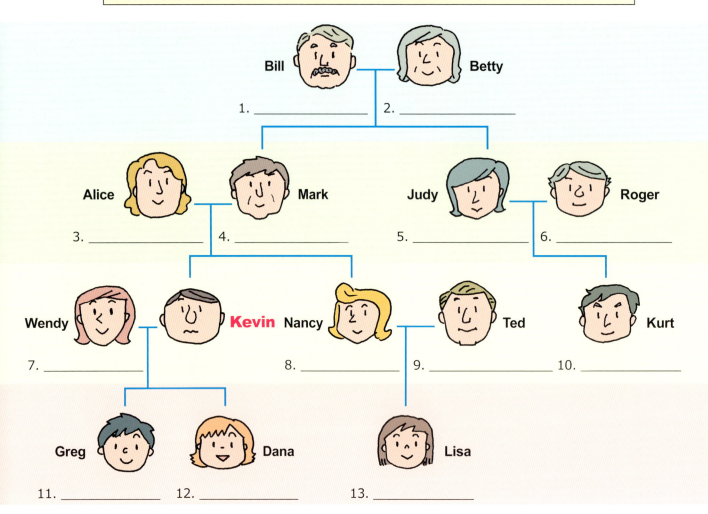

Part 2: Answer the questions below.　家系図について以下の質問に答えましょう。

1. Kevin is Kurt's _____ .
2. Greg is Nancy's _____ .
3. Kurt is Bill and Betty's _____ .
4. Betty is Alice's _____ .
5. Lisa is Wendy's _____ .

52

Unit 7　What's she like?

Practice 6

▶**Your Family Tree**　自分の家系図を書いてみよう

Draw your family tree. Then introduce your family to other members of your group. Describe their personality.
自分の家族関係を表す家系図を描いてグループのメンバーに紹介し，家族の性格も説明してみましょう。

Practice 7

▶**Writing**　ライティング

Write five sentences using different adjectives to talk about people you know.
5つの異なる形容詞を使って，友人や家族など知っている人を説明する文を作ってみましょう。

Example: My brother is kind.

1. _____ .
2. _____ .
3. _____ .
4. _____ .
5. _____ .

Unit 8

Do's and don'ts
していいことと悪いこと

Speaking スピーキング

Dialogue 1

Ms. Nakamura: Hikaru, no running around* during* naptime.
Hikaru: I'm not sleepy.
Ms. Nakamura: I understand, but you're making a lot of noise.*
Hikaru: Sorry.

Dialogue 2

Ms. Suzuki: Everyone, please be quiet. It's story time.
Shizuka: Shhhhh ...
Atsuko: Ms. Suzuki, please read "Cinderella" today!
Kenta: No! Read "Sleeping Beauty"!
Ms. Suzuki: Hey, what do you say when you ask for something?
Kenta: Can you PLEASE?

Dialogue 3

Mr. Fukuda: David, please pick up* your jacket and hang it up.*
David: Okay. Where can I hang it?
Mr. Fukuda: You can hang it by the door.
David: Can I hang my cap there, too?
Mr. Fukuda: Sure you can, but don't forget to take your things when you go home.

*run around 駆け回る　during 〜の間（期間）　noise 騒音　pick up ひろう
hang (hang up) 掛ける（電話を切る）

Unit 8   Do's and don'ts

Grammar

Imperative
命令文

All of the sentences below start with a verb. However, all English sentences must have a subject and a verb. What is the subject in these sentences?

以下の文はすべて動詞ではじまり，主語が省かれています。省かれている主語は何でしょう？

Put your hands in your lap.*   Don't trip.*
Wash your hands when you're done.   Don't push me.
Dry* your hands.   Don't talk.
Wait your turn.
Move over* a little.

一般動詞の原形を使うとき With general verbs   Come here.
Don't touch* it!

形容詞を使うとき With adjectives   Be quiet.   Be nice.

否定（〜してはダメ）と言いたいとき When you want to say "No!"

Don't を使うとき   Don't go outside.   Don't be shy.
No ~ing を使うとき   No looking.   No running.
Stop ~ing を使うとき   Stop laughing.   Stop fighting.

Adding "Please" makes sentences more polite. However, requests become even more polite if you start sentences with "Can you ~?" or "Would you ~?"

"Please" をつけると文が多少丁寧にはなりますが，何かしてほしいときは，"Can you ~?" や "Would you ~?" で文を始めるとより丁寧です。

Please get off* the swing.   Please be quiet.
Can you go down the slide?   Can you not talk?
Would you help clean up?   Would you not run?

* lap ひざ（腰から膝頭までの水平な部分）   trip つまずく   dry 乾かす   move over ずれる
touch さわる   get off 降りる

Textbook English vs. Real English

Textbook English	Real English
Please open the window. 窓を開けてください。 命令形に "Please" をつけると丁寧になる。	**Would you open the window?** 窓を開けていただけますか？ 丁寧に頼みたいときは Could/Can you ~? Would you ~? を使う。

Practice 1

▶ **Signs** 標識

Where would you see these signs? Write the correct letter from the box in the spaces below each sign.
以下の標識はどんな場所で見ることができますか？ 枠内から場所を選んで空欄に記号を記入しましょう。

A. Inside a restroom*
B. In a school hallway*
C. Near a swimming pool
D. At a school entrance*
E. At the entrance of a dangerous* area
F. On a train platform*
G. At a ticket window*
H. In a library
I. At a zoo
J. By a street corner
K. On a beach (with big waves)
L. In a park

1. _____

7. _____

2. _____

8. _____

3. _____

9. _____

4. _____

10. _____

5. _____

11. _____

6. _____

12. _____

*restroom トイレ　hallway ろうか　entrance 入口，玄関　dangerous 危険な，危ない
train platform 駅のホーム　ticket window 切符売り場　feed （動物などに）エサをやる
cross 横切る　line up 並ぶ　diving 飛び込み

Practice 2

▶ **Imperative** 命令文

Choose the correct expressions from the box and complete each sentence.
最も適切な表現を枠内から選び，文を完成させましょう。

> go outside 外に行く   come over こっちに来る   don't be shy 恥ずかしがらないで
> make a circle 円をつくる   take turns 順番にする，交代でする   don't touch 触らないで
> run around 駆け回る   run away 逃げる   stop fighting ケンカをやめる

1. Now introduce yourself to everyone in your new class. Speak loudly and clearly. _____ .

2. This paint is still wet. _____ it until it's dry.

3. It's story time. _____ here closer to me and _____ around me.

4. _____ right now! Be nice to each other and _____ playing with the toys.

5. It's a very nice day, so _____ and play in the playground.

6. Don't _____ the classroom. It's dangerous. And don't _____ from me when I'm talking to you. Stand here.

Practice 3

▶ **Complete the Sentences** 文を完成させよう

Write the correct verbs from the box in the spaces to complete the sentences.
最も適切な動詞を枠内から選んで空欄を埋め，文を完成させましょう。

> fight   put   be   make   spill こぼす
> leave 置いたままにする，置き忘れる   go   eat   run   touch   play

1. Don't _____ the toys on the floor. _____ them away.*

2. Don't _____ in the hallway.* It's dangerous, so walk please.

3. Johnny, _____ careful with your juice. Don't _____ it.

4. Don't _____ with each other. _____ nicely!

5. Don't _____ your painting. It's still wet.

6. Don't _____ a mess with your food. _____ carefully.

7. Don't _____ outside until it's recess.*

*put away 片づける   hallway ろうか   recess 休み時間

Practice 4

▶**What Will You Say?** 子供に何と言いますか？

What would you say to the children in the pictures? Choose the most appropriate sentence and write the letter under the pictures.

自分が先生や保護者だったら，子供の絵を見て何と言いますか？ 最も適当と思われる文を A～I から選び，絵の下に記入しましょう。

A. Can you stop whining?* D. Take a few more bites.* G. Make a circle around me.
B. Please be careful.* E. Stop fighting. H. Can you wipe your nose?*
C. Don't throw the book.* F. Don't make a mess with your toys. I. Take a shower.

*whine ぐずぐず言う　be careful 気をつける　throw 投げる　a bite ひとくち　wipe 拭く

1. _____   2. _____   3. _____

4. _____   5. _____   6. _____

7. _____   8. _____   9. _____

Practice 5

▶**Pair Work** ペアワーク

Explain what is happening in the pictures in **Practice 4**. You may want to use the words in the box.

枠内の単語を使って，Practice 4 の絵の状況を説明してみましょう。

Example: In picture one, the boy is playing in the mud.

runny nose 鼻水の出ている鼻　splashing water in a puddle 水たまりで水をまき散らす
complain 文句を言う　yell 叫ぶ　picky 好き嫌いのある

Unit 8　Do's and don'ts

Practice 6

▶**Mime Activity**　ジェスチャーゲーム

Your teacher will give you some cards with actions. Act out this action and have members of your group or class guess what you are doing. When guessing, ask questions like "Are you blowing your nose?*"

先生が様々な行動を表す単語が書かれたカードを渡します。その単語をもとに，あなたが何をしているのかグループのメンバーやクラスメイトに英語であててもらいましょう。あてる人は，"Are you blowing your nose?" など質問をしながらあててください。

＊ blow one's nose　〜の鼻をかむ

Practice 7

▶**Writing**　ライティング

Write two sentences using "Could you ~?" and two using "Would you ~?" using the pictures.

絵を見て"Could you ~?"を使った文を2つ，"Would you ~?"を使った文を2つ書いてみましょう。

Example: Could you throw away* the tissues?

1. _____ ?

2. _____ ?*

3. _____ ?

4. _____ ?

＊ throw away　捨てる　　go potty　トイレに行く

Practice 8

▶**Follow the Rules**　ルールを守ろう

Use the words in the box below to complete the list of rules.
以下の絵を見てどんなルールがあるのかを，枠内から単語を選んで書きましょう。

| follow 従う　walk　raise 挙げる　take　wash　listen　clean　share　run　talk　be |

1. _____ up the classroom.

2. Don't _____ . Please _____ .

3. _____ the dishes after eating.

4. _____ toys with others.

5. _____ to the teacher.

6. _____ your hand if you have a question.

Unit 8 Do's and don'ts

7. _____ quiet. Don't _____ in the library.

8. _____ off your shoes.

9. _____ the rules.

Practice 9

▶**Listening**　リスニング 48

Listen to the conversation and write in the missing words.　会話を聞いて空欄を埋めましょう。

Mr. Ito: It's _____ . Everyone, please _____

_____ .

Takuya: OK. Mr. Ito. Ai, _____ . I was _____ !

Mr. Ito: Ai, _____ .

Ai: But _____ .

Mr. Ito: I understand, but _____ .

Josh, _____ .

Josh: _____ .

Mr. Ito: You know there's _____ .

Practice 10

▶**Imperative Verbs** 命令文の動詞

Underline the verbs below. 動詞に下線を引いてみましょう。

49

Pat a cake, pat a cake, baker's man.
Bake me a cake as fast as you can.
Pat it and prick it and mark it with "B."
And put it in the oven for baby and me.

Pat it   Prick it   Mark it with

Review of Units 1 to 8
Unit 1 〜 8 までの復習

Practice 1　Complete the Sentences　文を完成させよう

Put the correct letters A ~ J in the spaces on the left to make sentences.
1 〜 10 までの空欄に入る最も適切なものを A 〜 J から選びましょう。

1. Please sit _____
2. Look _____
3. Please be _____
4. Face _____
5. Don't bend _____
6. Would you get _____
7. Don't _____
8. Can you put _____
9. Can you sit in _____
10. Please wash _____

A. the pages of your books.
B. on your shoes? We're going outside.
C. me, please. Don't turn away.*
D. run in the hallway!
E. down. Our lesson is starting.
F. your hands after you go to the toilet.
G. your musical instruments?*
H. quiet. No talking.
I. front of me? It's story time.
J. at me, please.

* face ~ 〜のほうに向く　　bend 曲げる　　turn away （顔を）そむける　　musical instruments 楽器
front (in front) 前方の（前の）

Practice 2

Expressing Feelings　感情を表そう

Write in the feelings you would have in the following situations. Refer to **Unit 6** for feeling words. Then share your answers in a group.
以下の状況ではどんな気持ちになりますか？　Unit 6 を参考にして文を完成させ，グループ内でみんなの答えを聞いてみましょう。

1. When I have a test, I feel _____ .
2. When I watch a baseball game, I feel _____ .
3. When I see a large dog walking towards me, I feel _____ .
4. When I'm in an airplane, I feel _____ .
5. When I arrive* to school on Monday morning, I feel _____ .
6. When my friend gets a high score on a test, I feel _____ .
7. When my friend gives me a birthday gift, I feel _____ .
8. When someone hits me, I feel _____ .

* arrive 到着する

Practice 3   Odd Word Out   仲間はずれを探そう

Circle the word that does not belong in each group. Then choose the title from the box below that best describes the group of words. The first one has been done for you.
各単語のグループでほかとは異なるものを選んで丸で囲み，残りの語群を表す題を枠内から選びましょう。

> Feelings   Playground activities   Languages   Family members
> Symptoms   School supplies   Personality*   ~~Places in a school~~

1. _Places in a school_
   classroom
   library
   playground
   (bedroom)

2. _____
   television
   backpack
   toothbrush
   Thermos

3. _____
   English
   Japanese
   India
   Chinese

4. _____
   fever
   cough
   dizzy
   hungry

5. _____
   sliding down a slide
   reading a book
   playing in a sandbox
   swinging on a swing

6. _____
   beautiful
   excited
   shocked
   nervous

7. _____
   delicious
   honest
   picky
   goofy

8. _____
   grandfather
   teacher
   cousin
   niece

*personality 性格

Practice 4   School Supplies and Stationery   学校で使う文房具

Write the words in the box under the correct picture.
次の絵に最も適切な単語を枠内から選びましょう。

Key Words 50

> scissors ハサミ   glue のり   Scotch tape セロテープ   stapler ホチキス
> ruler ものさし   paper clips ペーパークリップ   paint and paintbrush 絵の具と絵筆
> crayons クレヨン   color pencils 色えんぴつ   eraser 消しゴム
> pencil sharpener えんぴつ削り   highlighters 蛍光ペン   clay 粘土   stickers シール

Review of Units 1 to 8

1. _____ 2. _____ 3. _____ 4. _____

5. _____ 6. _____ 7. _____ 8. _____

9. _____ 10. _____ 11. _____ 12. _____

 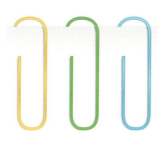

13. _____ 14. _____

Practice 5   Giving Directions   指示を出そう

Using the pictures and the words below, make sentences to give directions. The first has been done for you.

下の絵と語を見て「～しなさい」という文を作りましょう。

1. cut
2. open
3. put on
4. draw
5. brush
6. fold *

* fold たたむ，折る

1. <u>Cut the color paper</u>   .
2. _____ .
3. _____ .
4. _____ .
5. _____ .
6. _____ .

Review of Units 1 to 8

Practice 6 Crossword Puzzle クロスワードパズル

Work in pairs. **Student A** will stay on this page. **Student B** will turn to **Appendix 3**. Give hints to help your partner guess each word in your crossword below. When he/she guesses a word correctly, they should write it in their puzzle.

Student A はこのページを見てください。Student B は Appendix 3 を開いて、パートナーにクロスワードに入る単語をあてられるよう、英語でヒントをあげてください。わかったらその単語を書き入れましょう。

Example:
A: What is 19 down?
B: It is the opposite of "now."
A: Is it "then"?
B: Yes, that's it!

Student A

Unit 9

Let's eat lunch!
お昼を食べよう！

Speaking スピーキング

Dialogue 1
 51

- **Ms. Oliver:** It's lunchtime. Let's sit down and wait quietly.*
- **Matt:** I'm so hungry. I can't wait.
- **Ms. Oliver:** Let me give you paper napkins* first.
- **Matt:** What's for lunch today?
- **Ms. Oliver:** We will have curry and rice.
- **Matt:** That's my favorite,* but I don't like carrots.*
- **Ms. Oliver:** Let's not complain* so much about food.

Dialogue 2
 52

- **Makoto:** This meat is tough.*
- **Ms. Sasaoka:** Chew* it well so you don't choke* on it.
- **Makoto:** And this soup is hot.
- **Ms. Sasaoka:** Then wait for a few minutes.
- **Serina:** Can I have more cake? It was yummy.*
- **Ms. Sasaoka:** No, just one piece* for each person.

Dialogue 3
 53

- **Mr. Ishii:** Lunchtime is over. Let's clean up.
- **Ken:** Where do I put these dishes?
- **Mr. Ishii:** Put them over there.
- **Ken:** Where can I throw away* my cup?
- **Mr. Ishii:** It's paper, so throw it in that wastebasket.*

*wait 待つ　　napkin ナプキン　　favorite お気に入りの　　carrot ニンジン　　complain 文句を言う
tough かたい，丈夫な　　chew 噛（か）む　　choke のどを詰まらせる　　yummy おいしい
piece 一かけ，一切れ　　throw away 捨てる　　wastebasket ゴミ箱

 54

Grammar 1
Let's learn about "let"
let の使い方を学びましょう。

Let's ＋動詞の原形「〜しよう」
Let's clean up.
Let's all go outside.
Let's take a nap.

Let's not ＋動詞の原形「〜しないようにしよう」
Let's not run in the halls.
Let's not be so noisy.*
Let's not be selfish.*

*noisy うるさい
selfish わがままな

Unit 9　Let's eat lunch!

Practice 1

▶**Translation**　和文英訳

Translate the following sentences into English. Use the words in the box and the pictures to help you make your translations. Start the sentence with either "Let's" or "Let's not."

枠内の表現と絵を参考にして，下の文を英語にしましょう。"Let's" か "Let's not" で始めてください。

```
too much  いっぱい    sandcastle  砂のお城    play tag  鬼ごっこをする
pretend to be  〜になったふりをする    go outside  外に行く    superheroes  スーパーヒーロー
```

1. 鬼ごっこしよう。　_____.

2. あんまりいっぱい食べないようにしよう。　_____.

3. サッカーやろう。　_____.

4. スーパーヒーローになったふりしよう。　_____.

5. 外に行くのよそう。　_____.

6. 砂でお城を作ろう。　_____.

Practice 2

▶ **Listening**　リスニング

Listen to the following conversation and write in the missing words.
会話を聞いて空欄を埋めましょう。

Ms. Lee: It's _____ for _____ . _____ set the tables and _____ ready.* After you _____ hands, _____ to your seats.

Gary: I _____ !

Ms. Lee: _____ your hands.

Gary: See? They're _____ .

Ms. Lee: Your fingernails are* _____ .

Gary: But I _____ .

Ms. Lee: Go back and _____ .

Gina: Yuck!* _____ spinach.* And I _____ .

Ms. Lee: _____ so picky, Gina.

Remi: I can use chopsticks!*

Ms. Lee: _____ , Remi. _____ bowl. It might spill.*

* set the table テーブルに食事の用意をする　　get ready 準備する　　fingernail 手の指の爪
　Yuck! ゲーッ!　　spinach ホウレンソウ　　chopsticks お箸　　spill こぼす，こぼれる

Grammar 2
Different usages of "let"
let の異なる使い方――〜しよう，〜させる，〜してあげる

"Let's" is a contraction of "let us." When we use "let us" without a contraction, this often means "to permit" or "to offer" to do something.

Let's とは Let us の短縮形で，「〜しよう」という意味ですが，短縮せず Let us と使うとき，また us 以外の人（him, her など）が後に来る場合は，「〜しよう」という意味のほかに「〜させる」「〜してあげる」という意味にもなります。

Example:　Let's play with blocks.　　　　　　積み木で遊ぼう。
　　　　　　　Let us help you carry that table.　　そのテーブルを運ぶの手伝わせて（手伝ってあげる）。
　　　　　　　Let Yumi sleep a little more.　　　　ゆみちゃんをもう少し寝かせてあげよう。
　　　　　　　Let me go to the classroom with you.　教室に一緒に行ってあげる。

Practice 3

▶ **Writing** ライティング

You want to / don't want to do the following activities with your friend. Rewrite the sentences below, starting with "Let's" or "Let's not."
以下の行動をしたいか，したくないかを "Let's" または "Let's not" を使って書きかえましょう。

1. We want to go home.
   _____.

2. We don't want to play hide-and-seek.
   _____.

3. We don't want to fight anymore.
   _____.

4. We want to cook dinner together.
   _____.

5. We don't want to be late for school.
   _____.

Practice 4

▶ **Fill in the Blanks** 穴埋め問題

Choose the correct verbs in the box to complete the dialogue. You may need to change the verb to match the subject.
枠内から最も適切な動詞を選び，空欄を埋めましょう。必要なら動詞の形をかえてください。

| let (3 times)   want   get   be (3 times) |

Mr. Markle: It _____ time for music. Please _____ your instruments.

Victor: Yay! _____ us go and get them.

Mr. Markle: No running. I don't _____ you to fall.

Tetsuo: Hey! That _____ my tambourine.*

Mr. Markle: Don't fight. _____ us take turns, OK?

Tetsuo: But that's mine!

Mr. Markle: Tetsuo, _____ nice to Mayu. OK, now, _____ us practice* together.

* tambourine タンバリン   take turns 順番でする   practice 練習（する）

Practice 5

▶ Fill in the Blanks 穴埋め問題

Complete the following sentences using the translation and the words in the box. Use the pattern "let + person/thing + root verb."

枠内の単語を参考にして，以下の文を英語にしましょう。「let ＋人／もの＋動詞原形」を使って空欄を埋めてください。

take a look 見る　　play　　think about について考える　　cool down 冷める，冷ます　　talk to

1. _____ me _____ Ayumi to find out what happened.
    何があったのかあゆみに話してみるわ。

2. _____ me _____ at what you made.
    作ったもの見させて。

3. The soup is still very hot. _____ it _____ before you drink it.
    スープはまだとても熱いわ。飲む前に（それを）冷ましなさい。

4. That's a difficult question. _____ me _____ that for a bit.
    それは難しい問題です。少し（私に）考えさせてください。

5. Why don't you _____ Minh _____ with that toy?
    ミンちゃんにもそのオモチャで遊ばせてあげたら？

* find out （情報を）知る　　what happened 何が起こったのか

Practice 6

▶ Writing ライティング

Rewrite the following sentences with "Let me ~."

以下の英文を "Let me ~." を使って「～したい」を「～させて」という文にかえてみましょう。

Example: I want to help you. 手伝いたいの。 → Let me help you. 手伝わせて，手伝うわ。

1. I want to roll up your sleeves.
    _____.

2. I want to help you with your homework.
    _____.

3. I want to take a rest.
    _____.

4. I want to have a sip of your juice.
    _____.

5. I want to go to the restroom.
    _____.

* roll up まくる　　sleeves 袖　　take a rest 休む　　sip (a sip) ひとくちすする（ひとすすり）

Unit 9 Let's eat lunch!

Practice 7

▶**Scrambled Sentences** 文を並べ替えよう

Make a logical conversation by numbering the sentences from 1 to 6. Also, write T (for teacher) or S (for student).

文を並べ替えて会話の筋が通るように番号を入れましょう。T/S には T（teacher）か S（student）のどちらかを入れてください。

T/S	Number	
T	1	Yumi, you're not eating your carrots.
___	___	Eat some fried rice* then.
___	___	OK, Mr. Kimura, but just one bite. And I'll take out the carrots.
___	___	Yuck! I hate carrots. I don't want to eat them.
___	___	No! Fried rice has carrots.
___	___	Yumi, stop whining and try at least one bite of fried rice.

*fried rice チャーハン

Practice 8

▶**Role Play** ロールプレイ

Work in pairs. Write a dialogue between a teacher and a student about lunchtime and act out the dialogue. You may talk about the following topics in your role play.

以下のヒントを参考に，パートナーとランチタイムでの先生と生徒の会話を作り，実際にみんなの前で発表してみましょう。

- Washing hands
- Cleaning tables
- Today's menu
- Likes and dislikes
- Not complaining
- Making a mess

Unit 10

What do you want to do?

何したい？

Speaking スピーキング

Dialogue 1

 57

Ken: What do you want to do?
Mari: Let's go outside and play!
Ken: Okay, I want to play in the sandbox. I'll get a bucket* and a shovel.*
Mari: I don't want to play in the sandbox. I want to go on the swings.
Ken: Then can we play in the sandbox after the swings?
Mari: Sure.

Dialogue 2

58

Mr. Kent: What are you looking for?
Junko: I want to cut out* some pictures. Is that OK?
Mr. Kent: You sure can.*
Junko: But I don't know where the scissors are.
Mr. Kent: They're in the top drawer.*
Junko: Oh, here they are.*
Mr. Kent: Put them back* when you're finished.
Junko: OK. Ouch!
Mr. Kent: What's wrong?*
Junko: I cut my finger.

* bucket バケツ　shovel シャベル　cut out 切り抜く　You sure can. もちろん（やって）いいよ。
drawer 引き出し　Here they are. あっ，あった。　put ~ back ～を元（の位置）に戻す
What's wrong? どうしたの？

Unit 10 What do you want to do?

Culture Note: Playing with Friends

Many Japanese students use the word "play" for going out or spending time with their friends. In English, the expression "I play with my friends" would only be used among small children, not among adults. For young adult activities, it would be better to use "hang out" or "go out."

日本の学生は，友達と出かけることを英語で言い表すときに，"play" を使うことがよくありますが，"play" は英語では小さな子供の遊びを表すときにしか使われません。大人同士で出かけたり，時間を過ごしたりするときには，"hang out" か "go out" を使いましょう。

We're hanging out   We're playing

Grammar

want/wants to ~ ＝ ～したい   **don't/doesn't want to ~ ＝ ～したくない**

I want to play in the sandbox.   I don't want to play in the sandbox.

I want to go on the swings.   I don't want to go on the swings.

Key Words

Playground Words

play in the sandbox 砂場で遊ぶ　　dig a hole 穴を掘る　　make a tunnel トンネルをつくる
climb the tree 木に登る　　go on the swing ブランコに乗る　　go on the slide すべり台に乗る
slide down the slide すべり台を滑り降りる　　get on the seesaw, ride the seesaw シーソーに乗る
play on the monkey bars うんていをする　　play tag 鬼ごっこをする　　play hide-and-seek かくれんぼをする
play hopscotch けんけんぱをする　　play catch キャッチボールをする　　play tic-tac-toe まるばつをする
play kick-the-can 缶けりをする　　do cat's cradle あやとりをする　　jump rope なわとび（をする）

Practice 1

▶ **Writing** ライティング

Look at the actions in the pictures and then write sentences using the words in parentheses.
（　　）内の語を使って，絵に合った文を書きましょう。

1. _____ (I, want)

2. _____ (let, us)

3. _____ (we, want)

4. _____ (let, us)

5. _____ (we, want)

6. _____ (let's)

Practice 2

▶ **Pair Work**   ペアワーク

Imagine you and your partner are children. You and your partner want to do different things. Using the words in the "Playground Words" on page 76, complete the dialogue below and practice with your partner.

子供になったつもりでパートナーと会話を作りましょう。お互い別の遊びがしたいことを相手に伝えます。76 ページの "Playground Words" のリストを使って会話を作りましょう。

A: Let's _____!

B: I don't want to _____.

　 I want to _____.

A: OK. Can we _____ first and then _____?

B: Sure. But first, I need to _____.

Practice 3

▶ **Writing**   ライティング

Imagine you are a teacher. What would you say to children in the following situations? Choose the most appropriate expressions from the box.

あなたが先生だったらこんなとき何と言いますか？ 枠内の表現を使って子供たちに話しかける文を作りましょう。

Key Expressions: Let's take turns.「順番, 順番。」　Be patient.「我慢しなさい。」　Wait. / You need to wait.「待って。」
Hold on.「ちょっと待って。」　What do you say?「(こんなとき) なんて言うの？」
Slow down.「あわてないで。」　Calm down.「落ち着きなさい。」　Be nice.「やさしくね。」
Take it easy.「落ち着いてよ。」「じゃあね。」　Be careful!「気をつけてね！」

1. Jack is crying and screaming.*
   _____

2. Yuka is swinging. Reiko comes too close to the swing.
   _____

3. Risa is on top of the slide. Two boys are telling her to hurry up.*
   _____

4. Ryan complains that Mei isn't letting him use the toy. Mei says she wants to use it for a few minutes first.
   _____

5. Yuka wants to join* hide-and-seek, but Ami told her, "No, we don't want to play with you!"
   _____

6. Atsushi is running to get a toy.
   _____

7. Sara tells you, "I want a cookie!"
   _____

*scream 叫ぶ　　hurry up 急ぐ　　join 参加する

Practice 4

▶**Pair Work**　ペアワーク

Take turns making sentences using some of the following expressions in the box and looking at the pictures.

パートナーと順番に，枠内の表現を使って絵に合った文を作りましょう。

Key Words

pull 引く　　push 押す　　pick up 迎えに行く／来る，ひろう　　put on 着る　　take off 脱ぐ pull up 持ち上げる　　pull down（引き）降ろす　　bend 曲げる　　stretch 伸ばす　　lend 貸す　　borrow 借りる get on 乗る　　get off 降りる　　hurry up 急ぐ　　slow down ゆっくりさせる　　win 勝つ　　lose 負ける，なくす find 見つける　　turn on スイッチを入れる，蛇口などを開ける　　turn off スイッチを切る，蛇口などを閉める

Example: Turn on the light.

1. _____　2. _____　3. _____

5. Recess is over. _____

4. _____　_____　6. _____ your arms.

Practice 5

▶**Mime Activity**　ジェスチャーゲーム

In a group, take turns miming the verbs (**Key Words**) in **Practice 4**. The other students should guess what is being mimed.

Practice 4 の枠内にある動詞をジェスチャーで表して，パートナーにあててもらいましょう。

Practice 6

▶ **Opposites** 反対語

Choose the adjective with the opposite meaning from the box and write it in the chart below.
1～12までの形容詞と反対の意味の単語を枠内から選んで書きましょう。

Key Words 63

| difficult 難しい   empty 空の   early 早い   far 遠い   right 正しい   near 近い   noisy うるさい |
| dry 乾いた   full いっぱい   smooth なめらかな   clean 清潔な   dirty 汚い   easy 簡単な   late 遅い |
| exciting わくわくする   wrong 間違った   wet 濡れた   loose ゆるい   safe 安全な   quiet 静かな |
| dangerous 危険な   rough 粗い，ざらざらした   tight（服などが）きつい   boring つまらない |

Adjectives	Adjectives with Opposite Meaning	Adjectives	Adjectives with Opposite Meaning
1. quiet		7. early	
2. smooth		8. near	
3. wet		9. full	
4. clean		10. safe	
5. easy		11. tight	
6. exciting		12. right	

Practice 7

▶ **Choose the Best Sentence** あとに続く文を選ぼう

Read the sentences on the left. Choose the best second sentence on the right and write the letters in the space.
1～8までの文に続く最も適切な文をA～Hの中から選んで空欄に記入しましょう。

1. Don't play with the knife. _____
2. Don't shout or scream. _____
3. I waited here for 30 minutes. _____
4. I couldn't finish all the math homework. _____
5. I ate too much. _____
6. I got 100 on my test. _____
7. Change your clothes.* _____
8. I spilled juice on the floor. _____

A. It was too difficult.
B. They're dirty.
C. I'm really full.*
D. You're too noisy.
E. I got all the answers right.
F. Be careful, because it's wet.
G. You're late.
H. It's dangerous.

*full（お腹などが）いっぱい　change clothes 着替える

79

Textbook English vs. Real English

Reaction Sounds, Words, and Expressions.
英語であいづちをうつ

How do you respond to show that you're listening to someone? Don't just move your head. Respond with appropriate sounds and expressions.
質問でない意見にどう反応しますか？ うなずいたり首を振ったりするだけでなく，きちんと声を出して「聞いている」ということを表しましょう。

Textbook English	Real English

Responding to statements:
   I see.
 	
 Responding to questions:
   Well ... let me see.
	Uh-huh.
	 Really?
	 Oh no!
	 Aww!
	 Wow!
	 Whoa!*
	 Ummm ...

* whoa[wóu]! うわっ！

Practice 8

▶**Reaction Words**　あいづち

Use the words and expressions in the box on page 81 to react to the following situations. Use different words and expressions each time.
次の状況に対してどのような反応をしますか？ それぞれ異なるあいづち表現を枠内から選んで記入しましょう。

Key Words

Oh boy! えー！ あらー！　　Wow!　　Great!　　Oops! おっと！　　Ow! / Ouch! 痛い！
What!?　　Oh no!　　No way! うそー！　　Yuck! ゲー！　　I'm so sorry.
Oh my gosh! / Gosh! / Gee!　　Are you kidding? うそでしょ？　　That's amazing! すごい！

1. **Teacher:** OK, everybody. Take out your pencils. I'm giving you a surprise test.

   Reaction: _____

2. **Teacher:** Take out your textbooks! Haruki, where's your textbook?

   Reaction: _____ I forgot it at home.

3. **Friend:** I won a singing contest. I'm going to be on TV!

   Reaction: _____

4. **Teacher:** Don't spill any paint on the floor.

   Reaction: _____ I just spilled some.

5. **Doctor:** I'm going to give you a shot. This is going to hurt.

   Reaction: _____ That really hurt!

6. **Parent:** You don't like this natto ice cream, do you?

   Reaction: _____ It's terrible!

7. **Friend:** I got 100 on my math test.

   Reaction: _____

8. **Friend:** I just met a famous Korean pop star. He invited me to Korea to visit him.

   Reaction: _____

9. **Friend:** Here's a birthday present I got for you.

   Reaction: _____

10. **Friend:** My grandfather is very sick. He just went into the hospital.

    Reaction: _____

11. **Mother:** We're having cake for dessert.

    Reaction: _____

12. **Teacher:** Mika, what's your phone number?

    Reaction: _____ I forget.

Textbook English vs. Real English

Exclamatory Sentence （感嘆文）

You can express exclamatory sentences by simply adding an adjective after "How."
感嘆文を作るときは，通常 "How" のあとに形容詞をつけるだけで OK です。

Textbook English (Long)	Real English (short)
感嘆文（なんて〜なんだ！）を使う場合	How のあとは形容詞のみで感嘆文を表す。
How＋形容詞＋主語＋動詞！	How＋形容詞！
How beautiful that flower is! →	How beautiful!　なんてきれいなの！
How exciting the game was! →	How exciting!　それはわくわくするね！
How sad that is! →	How sad!　それは悲しいね！

Practice 9

▶**How Wonderful!**　なんてステキなの！

Write exclamatory sentences with "How ...!" using the pictures and the hints in parentheses.
カッコ内のヒントと絵を参考にして，"How" ではじまる感嘆文を作りましょう。

Example:
　　Long:　How beautiful that/the present is!
　　Short:　How beautiful!

1. Long: _____ !
　 Short: _____ !
　 (wonderful ... is)

2. Long: _____ !
　 Short: _____ !
　 (exciting ... was)

Unit 10 — What do you want to do?

3. Long: _____!
   Short: _____!
   (scary ... was)

4. Long: _____!
   Short: _____!
   (sad ... is)

Unit 11

What do you have to do?
何をしなければならないの？

Speaking スピーキング

Dialogue 1

Mr. Kawano: OK everyone, what do we have to do before lunch?
Kenta: We have to wash our hands.
Mr. Kawano: That's right. Hurry up.
Junko: Do we have to gargle* too?
Mr. Kawano: No, you don't have to.

Dialogue 2

Ms. Jiken: OK, everyone, make a line.* Tony, you mustn't push.
Tony: But I was first in line.* Cara shouldn't cut in line.*
Ms. Jiken: Cara, let Tony be first. Everyone should wait for their turn.*
Cara: But I need to go to the bathroom.
Ms. Jiken: Then hurry up and go.

Dialogue 3

Mr. Blake: Can we talk tomorrow instead of today?
Mr. Kato: I'm at school tomorrow, so it shouldn't be a problem.
Mr. Blake: I think I have a fever, so I should probably go see a doctor.
Mr. Kato: In that case,* you should go right now. It's better you don't stay in school if you're sick.

*gargle うがいをする　　make a line 列をつくる　　first in line 一番先　　cut in line 列に割り込む
　　wait for (one's) turn （人の）番を待つ　　in that case その場合

Unit 11 What do you have to do?

Grammar
Modal Verbs
助動詞

Soft

It stopped raining, so we **can** go outside and play now.
It's raining, so we **can't** (cannot) go outside yet.
Can/May I go to the bathroom? Yes, you **can/may**.
You **should** eat your vegetables.
You **shouldn't** (should not) wear your indoor shoes in the playground.
Your pants are wet, so you **ought to** change them.
You **have to** wash your hands before lunch.
You don't **have to** wear a coat today. It's warm.
You **need to** bring an extra pair of underwear.
Your parents **must** sign this form* if you want to go on the field trip.*
You **mustn't** (must not) push other kids when you're on the slide. It's dangerous.

Strong

* form 書式，用紙   field trip 遠足

Practice 1

▶ **Complete the Sentences** 文を完成させよう

Complete the sentences below with the words in the box.
枠内の表現を使って，以下の1～8の文を完成させましょう。

| can (use three times)   must   mustn't (use two times)   should (use two times)   shouldn't |

1. Student: _____ I take a nap? I'm sleepy.

   Teacher: Wait just 10 minutes. Then it's naptime and you _____ sleep.

2. You _____ bring a permission slip* from your parents if you want to go on the school field trip.

3. You _____ dive* into the swimming pool. It's not deep, so it's dangerous.

4. If you're not feeling well, you _____ go home early if you want.

5. You _____ eat too much. You might get a stomachache.

6. If you wet your pants, you _____ change them or they will be stinky.*

7. Timmy, you _____ hit Susie. You may hurt her.

8. That's a beautiful picture, Emily. You _____ be an artist.

* permission slip 許可書   dive 飛び込む   stinky 臭い

Practice 2

▶**Writing** ライティング

Ask your partner if she/he has to do the following things. Complete the answers using "don't."
パートナーに 1〜5 の質問をし，例文を参考に "don't" を使って会話を作りましょう。

> **Example:** A: Do you have to see your teacher?
> B: Yes, but I don't have to see her today.

1. A: Do you have to go shopping?
   B: Yes, but I _____ shopping until tomorrow.

2. A: Do you have to do your homework?
   B: Yes, but I _____ it right now.

3. A: Do you have to buy milk?
   B: Yes, but I _____ eggs.

4. A: Do you have to eat vegetables* every day?
   B: Yes, but I _____ a lot every day.

5. A: Do I have to wear a tie tomorrow?
   B: Yes, but you _____ a coat.

*vegetables 野菜

Practice 3

▶**Pair Work** ペアワーク

Take turns asking and answering the following questions. Give "true" answers.
お互いに以下の質問をして答えましょう。

1. Do you have to do homework today?
2. Do you have to make dinner tonight?
3. Do you have to get up early tomorrow morning?
4. Do you have to come to school on Saturday?
5. Do you have to do chores* at home?

*chores 家事，雑用

Unit 11　**What do you have to do?**

Practice 4

▶**Listening**　リスニング 71

Listen to the following message from a teacher and write in the missing words.
先生から保護者へのメッセージを聞いて，空欄を埋めましょう。

Message to Parents

It's summer now and the weather* is getting _____.
Children _____ a lot of clothes. They _____ to school. They _____ wear their coats to school. Children _____ when they play outside at our school. They _____ plenty of* water. After school, children _____ activities if it is over 30 degrees.* However, children _____ in air-conditioned* rooms for too long or drink _____ drinks.

＊weather 天気　　plenty (of) たくさんの，十分な　　degree 度
　air conditioner (air-conditioned) エアコン（エアコンの効いた）

Practice 5

▶ **Using Modals**   助動詞を使おう

Look at the pictures below and write sentences using the modals shown in **Grammar** on page 85. Use your imagination.

85ページのGrammarにある助動詞を使い，下の絵の状況を想像して説明しましょう。

Example: You should take turns.

1.

2.

3.

4.

5.

6.

7.

8.

9.

10.

1. _____ .
2. _____ .
3. _____ .
4. _____ .
5. _____ .
6. _____ .
7. _____ .
8. _____ .
9. _____ .
10. _____ .

Practice 6

▶ **Group Work**　グループワーク

Work in groups. Share your sentences in **Practice 5** with members of your group. Help each other by correcting mistakes.

Practice 5 で作った文をグループで直し合いましょう。

Practice 7

▶ **Running Dictation**　ランニングディクテーション

You will now do a dictation exercise. Work in groups. There are sentences posted around the classroom. Take turns running to a sentence, reading it silently, returning to your group, and whispering to a writer. Write each sentence below. Then order the sentences from 1 to 9 and write "T" for teacher and "S" for student.

教室内にいろいろな文が貼ってあります。各グループのひとりが貼ってある文を読みに行き，その文をグループのメンバーに口頭で伝えたものを書きましょう。"number"の欄にはストーリーの順番を，"T/S"の欄には T ＝先生か S ＝生徒かのどちらかを入れてください。

Number	T/S	Sentences
_____	____	_____
_____	____	_____
_____	____	_____
_____	____	_____
_____	____	_____
_____	____	_____
_____	____	_____
_____	____	_____
_____	____	_____

Practice 8

▶ **Writing**　ライティング

Look at the pictures below. Make sentences using "Can you tell me why S + V?" Make sure you are using the correct verb tense.

次の絵を見て，"Can you tell me why S + V?" を使って「なぜ〜したのか教えてくれる？」という文を作ってください。動詞は適切な時制に直しましょう。

Example: Can you tell me why you're sad?

1.　　　　2.　　　　3.　　　　4.

1. _____?
2. _____?
3. _____?
4. _____?

Practice 9

▶ **Pair Work**　ペアワーク

Read the dialogue below. Then choose one of the pictures from **Practice 8** and write your own dialogue. After you have done, remember your dialogue and prepare to act it out in front of the class.

次の会話を読み，Practice 8 の絵からひとつを選んで自分でオリジナルの会話を作ってみましょう。会話ができたら暗記して，みんなの前で演じてみましょう。

Ms. Mori: Lyn, can you tell me why you pushed Saki?
Lyn: Saki pushed me first!
Ms. Mori: Saki, did you?
Saki: Yeah, but Lyn took my book away.
Ms. Mori: Can you both apologize* to each other?
Lyn: Sorry.
Saki: Sorry.
Ms. Mori: Now, you must get along with* each other.

* apologize　あやまる　　get along with　仲良くする

Unit 11   What do you have to do?

Practice 10

▶**Pair Work**   ペアワーク
Look at the pictures below and make sentences using the words.
それぞれの絵を参考にし，単語を並べ替えて正しい文を作ってみましょう。

> **Example:** hear / saying / what / you / can't / I / what / are
> <u>I can't hear what you are saying.</u>

1. are / what / can't / I / saying / you / understand
   _____.

2. what / can't / I / you / believe / did
   _____.

3. tell / I / you / what / heard / can't / I
   _____.

   It's a secret.

4. what / making / look at / I'm / can't / you
   _____.

   It's a surprise.

91

Unit 12
I need to go potty
トイレに行きたい

Speaking スピーキング

Dialogue 1 72

- **Ms. Bridges:** Who needs to go potty?*
- **Yuri:** I do! I need to go poo.*
- **Mikey:** Me, too.
- **Ms. Bridges:** You can go by yourselves, right?
- **Yuri:** Yes. I'm fine.
- **Mikey:** Me, too.
- **Ms. Bridges:** And don't forget to wipe* your bottom.*

Dialogue 2 73

- **Chris:** I need to go pee.*
- **Ms. Bridges:** There's no toilet here. Can you wait a few minutes?
- **Chris:** No, I have to go now.
- **Ms. Bridges:** OK. Go inside and see Mr. Yamaguchi. He can show you where to go.

*potty (go potty) トイレ（トイレに行く）　poo うんち　wipe 拭く
bottom おしり，すそ　pee おしっこ

Unit 12 I need to go potty

Practice 1

▶ **Writing** ライティング

Give directions to parents about what to bring to the following occasions. Think of other occasions and what things children need to bring.
以下の行事があるときに，持って来るものについて保護者に連絡します。その他の行事に必要なものも考えてみましょう。

1. **First day of swimming**

    Please bring _____

    _____ .

2. **Field trip**

    Please bring _____

    _____ .

3. **Sports day**

    Please bring _____

    _____ .

Grammar 1

Make Sure
必ず～する

 74

"Make sure* + S + V" means someone wants to give an important reminder to the other person.
"Make sure S + V" の表現は「Sが必ずVするように」という意味です。

Make sure you wash your hands.

Make sure your parents fill-out* this form.

＊ make sure 必ず～する　　fill-out 記入する

Practice 2

▶Writing ライティング

Following is a note to parents from their child's school.
以下は子供の学校から保護者にあてたメッセージです。

> Please make sure your child has the following* things on the first day of school, and label* all of your child's belongings.*
> - A change of underwear,* shirt, and pants
> - If your child is not toilet-trained,* bring at least 4 or 5 extra* pairs of pants, and underwear.
> - An extra pair of socks and shoes
> - A futon and a blanket* for naptime
> - Children must wear sneakers. Sandals and flip-flops* often cause* injuries.*

*following 以下の　　label 名前をつける　　belongings 持ち物　　change of underwear 下着の替え
toilet-trained オムツがとれた　　extra 追加の　　blanket 毛布　　flip-flops ビーチサンダル
cause 引き起こす　　injury ケガ

Write questions regarding the note above. Use the following verbs in the box to write questions.
上記の連絡事項について、枠内の動詞を使った質問を作ってみましょう。

> bring 持って来る　　need 必要とする　　prepare 準備をする
> wear 着る　　have to / has to しなければならない

Example: Do I have to bring a pillow?

1. 予備の靴を持って来なければいけませんか？（予備の靴＝ an extra pair of shoes）

    Do I have to _____?

2. 下着はいつ必要ですか？

    When do I _____?

3. 替えのパンツを4，5枚用意しなければならないのは誰ですか？

    Who needs to _____?

4. 子供たちはビーチサンダルをはいてもいいですか？

    Can the children _____?

5. なぜ子供たちはスニーカーをはかなくてはなりませんか？

    Why do children _____?

Practice 3

▶**Pair Work** ペアワーク

Now take turns asking and answering questions with a partner using information from the note in **Practice 2**, as in the example below.
例文にあるように，Practice 2 のメッセージを参考にして順番に質問を作り，パートナーに聞いてみましょう。

> **Example:** Parent: Do I have to bring a pillow?   Teacher: No, you don't.
> Parent: What do I need for naptime?   Teacher: A futon and a blanket.

Practice 4

▶**Writing** ライティング

Use the verbs in the box to complete the sentences below with the two imperative forms shown in the example. Notice that "Make sure to + V" can replace "Make sure that S + V." They have the same meaning.
例文を参考にして，枠内の動詞を使って2種類の命令文を作りましょう。"Make sure that S + V" は，"Make sure to + V" でも表せます。

> **Example:** Make sure **that** you wash your hands.
> Make sure **to** wash your hands.

| drink   show   arrive   lock   go   wash   brush   bring |

1. Make sure that _____ your teeth after lunch.
2. Make sure that _____ by 8 a.m. tomorrow.
3. Make sure to _____ your swimsuit tomorrow.
4. Make sure to _____ your hands before lunch.
5. Make sure that _____ the door when you leave the house.
6. Make sure to _____ the message book* to your parents.
7. Make sure that _____ lots of water when it's hot.
8. Make sure to _____ to the restroom if you need to go potty.

* message book 連絡帳

Grammar 2
"Can/Could" Used for Requests
"Can/Could" を使って「〜してくれる？」

Instead of using the imperative form, we can use "Can you ~?" or "Could you ~?"
命令文を使う代わりに，"Can you ~?" や "Could you ~?" という表現を使ってみましょう。

A: Can anyone tell me what we have to do before a nap?

B: Brush our teeth.

A: That's right! Now, can you go and brush your teeth and get ready for a nap?

B: I can't find my toothbrush.

A: Oh, your mom brought a new one today and took the old one back. Here you are.

Practice 5

▶ **Pair Work**　ペアワーク

In pairs, practice making requests using "Can you ~?" and "Could you ~?" using the pictures below.
何かをしてほしいときに，"Can you ~?" "Could you ~?"「〜をしてくれる？」という文を使って聞いてみましょう。

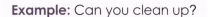
Example: Can you clean up?

1.

2.

3.

4.

5.

6.

Unit 12   I need to go potty

Practice 6

▶ **Complete the Sentences** 文を完成させよう

Choose the correct words from the box to complete the sentences. Be sure to use the verbs in the correct tense.
枠内の単語を使って文を完成させましょう。動詞を適切な時制に直して使ってください。

Key Words

| wipe 拭く   laundry machine 洗濯機   sip ひとすすり (use twice) |
| huge 巨大な   pile 山積み   dirty 汚れた   laundry 洗濯   drip たれる |

76

Yuri: Mommy, can I have a _____ of your juice?

Mother: OK, but just a small _____ , OK?

Yuri: OK. (Starts to drink juice ...)

Mother: Yuri, you _____ some! Your mouth and chin are _____.
_____ them with this napkin.

Yuri: My T-shirt is wet! My pants, too!

Mother: Don't worry. Take them off and put them over there by the _____
_____ . There is a _____ _____ of dirty
clothes there. I'll do the _____ this morning.

Yuri: OK. Sorry Mommy.

Practice 7

▶ **Listening** リスニング

77

Listen to the following conversation and write in the missing words. 会話を聞いて空欄を埋めましょう。

Ms. Suzuki: It's time _____ ! Let's _____ ,
everyone. Ken, are you OK? You look _____.

Ken: I can't find _____ .

Ms. Suzuki: _____ your cubby?*

Ken: Yes, _____ . Maybe I forgot _____
back from home.

Ms. Suzuki: Oh, I see. We have an extra set of pajamas, so _____
that today.

Ken: I don't want to wear that! That's _____ .
I'm _____ in my underwear.

Ms. Suzuki: Well, _____ today, so I guess* that's OK.

* cubby 小さな収納スペース   guess あてる

Practice 8

▶**Writing** ライティング

Make sentences using the expression "It's time to ~." Then, think of an extra sentence using the imperative form.
次の表現を使って "It's time to ~." 「～する時間です。」という文を作り，そのあとに来る命令文をひとつ考えてみましょう。

> **Example:** It's time to brush your teeth. Get your toothbrush and toothpaste.

1. practice a song
   _____

2. play outside
   _____

3. eat lunch
   _____

4. clean up
   _____

5. take a nap
   _____

6. go home
   _____

Practice 9

▶**Translation** 和文英訳

Translate the following sentences into English. Use "try to ~" and "try not to ~." Use present continuous for 1 and 2 and the imperative for 3 and 4.
"try to ~"「～しようとする」，"try not to ~"「～しないようにする」を使って以下の文を英語にしましょう。1，2は現在進行形を，3，4は命令形を使ってください。

Examples:
Present continuous: The boy is trying not to cry.
男の子は泣かないように頑張っている。
Imperative: Try not to cry. 泣かないように頑張って。

Unit 12　I need to go potty

1. 男の子は木に登ろうとしてる。
   _____

2. 女の子はチョウチョを捕まえようとしてる。
   _____

3. 膝を曲げないようにね。
   _____

4. お水をこぼさないようにね。
   _____

Practice 10

▶**Group Work**　グループワーク

Share your memories with other students in your group.
グループ内で以下のような思い出について話しあってみましょう。

 A scary memory.
 A funny memory.
 A happy memory.

Unit 13
Good job!
よくやったね!

Speaking スピーキング

Dialogue 1 78

- **Tetsuo:** I drew a picture. Take a look,* Ms. Sakai!
- **Ms. Sakai:** Wow! How pretty! You did a good job!* It's so colorful!
- **Tetsuo:** I want to draw another one. Do you have more paper?
- **Ms. Sakai:** I sure do. Here.

Dialogue 2 79

- **Mr. Meadows:** That's a really nice blouse you're wearing, Etsuko.
- **Etsuko:** Thanks. Mommy bought it for me.
- **Mr. Meadows:** Oh, you're lucky. It's so pretty.
- **Etsuko:** Look at the cat I made from clay.
- **Mr. Meadows:** Well done.* You did a good job.

Dialogue 3 80

- **Mana:** Can I have some paper? I want to paint.
- **Ms. Saito:** Oh, no! We don't have any more paper.
- **Tetsuo:** You can help me paint* my picture, Mana.
- **Ms. Saito:** Thank you for sharing, Tetsuo. That's very nice of you.

*take a look 見る　　good job よくやったね　　well done よくできたね　　paint 絵を描く

Unit 13 Good job!

Grammar
Past Tense 1
過去形1

 81

Past Action	Teacher's Compliment
I drew a picture.	You did a good job.
I gave Tina a present.	That was very nice of you.
I put all the toys away.	Well done.
I gave my book to Haruna.	Thank you for sharing.

Practice 1

▶ **Giving a Compliment**   ほめてあげよう

How would you compliment children in the following situations in the classroom? Choose the most appropriate compliment from the box.
1～6の状況ではどのように子供をほめてあげますか？ A～Fの中から最も適切なものを選びましょう。

A. Wow! What a big boy you are!
B. Nice job! That looks very pretty.
C. Thank you! You were such a great help!
D. That's very thoughtful of you to share like that!
E. Wow, that looks nice. It must be warm, too.
F. You guys* sounded wonderful!

1. Kaito shared his book with Miyu.　_____
2. Kei helped you clean up the table after lunch.　_____
3. All the students in class sang a song well.　_____
4. Jason tied his shoelaces* all by himself.*　_____
5. Dana has a new winter coat.　_____
6. Ken painted a nice picture.　_____

*guys あなたたち   shoelaces 靴ひも   by himself/herself 彼／彼女 ひとりで

Practice 2

▶ Past Tense 過去形

Write the past tense of the following verbs. 以下の動詞の過去形を書きましょう。

Regular verbs 規則変化をする動詞

try _____   share _____   want _____

start _____   tie _____   talk _____

Irregular verbs 不規則変化の動詞

do _____   sing _____   know _____

wear _____   go _____   have _____

get _____   make _____   say _____

Practice 3

▶ Complete the Conversation 会話を完成させよう

Choose the correct words from the box to complete the conversation.
枠内から適切な表現を選んで空欄を埋めましょう。

> How did ~ go? ～はどうだった？ うまく行った？   How nice! なんてすてき！
> I knew it! やっぱり！ 思った通り！   wore "wear"「着る」の過去形
> make mistakes 間違う   purple むらさき色（の）   recital 発表会   You did it! やったね！

Ms. Ito: You had a piano _____ yesterday, right? _____
_____ it _____ ?

Risa: It went great! I didn't _____ any _____ .

Ms. Ito: _____ _____ _____ ! You play the piano so well.

Risa: Yes, but I was afraid at first. I didn't want to play.

Ms. Ito: But _____ _____ _____ !

Risa: Yes, I did. And I _____ a _____ dress.

Ms. Ito: You did? Oh, _____ _____ ! That's your favorite* color!

* favorite お気に入りの

Practice 4

▶ **Questions in Past Tense** 過去形の質問文

Ask your partner questions using the expression "Did you ~?" and using the verbs in the box. Take turns asking questions.

枠内の動詞を使って，パートナーに"Did you ~?"「～しましたか？」と聞いてみましょう。聞かれたら"Yes"か"No"で答えてください。

| finish | eat | see | watch | clean | take a shower | wash | do |

Example: A: Did you finish today's homework?
B: Yes, I did.

Practice 5

▶ **Complete the Conversation** 会話文を完成させよう

Change the verbs in the sentences below to the appropriate tense. Most are past tense.

カッコ内の動詞を適切な時制にかえて空欄を埋めましょう。ほとんどの文は過去形になります。

Eric: Ms. Kato, I _____ (walk) all the way from home today!

Ms. Kato: You _____ (do)? You _____ (do not come) by car today?

Eric: No, because my dad _____ (need) the car, so Mommy and I _____ (decide*) to walk.

Ms. Kato: Good for you! How long _____ (do) it _____ (take)?

Eric: It _____ (take) only 20 minutes. I _____ (be) sweaty now, though.

Ms. Kato: I see. _____ (do) you want to _____ (drink) some water?

Eric: Yes, I do.

* decide 決める

Practice 6

▶**Matching** あいづちを探そう

Choose the most appropriate response for 1 ~ 5 by writing the correct letter in the spaces.
1～5の文の反応として最も適切なものを，A～Eの中から選んで記入しましょう。

> A. Oh, how fun! What animals did you see?
> B. Boy,* that was fast!
> C. How was it? Do you think you passed?*
> D. Were they delicious?
> E. Good for you! Let me hear you.

1. I had a test yesterday.   _____
2. I already cleaned all my paintbrushes.   _____
3. My mother made pancakes yesterday.   _____
4. I went to the zoo with my dad.   _____
5. Ms. Terada, I can count from one to 10!   _____

*Boy! わぁー！   pass 合格する

Practice 7

▶**Listening** リスニング   82

Listen and write in the missing verbs. 以下の童謡を聞いて空欄を埋めましょう。

This Little Piggy

This little piggy _____ to the market.

This little piggy _____ home.

This little piggy _____ roast beef.

This little piggy _____ none.

This little piggy _____ "wee wee wee" _____ _____

_____ _____ .

104

Practice 8

▶**What Did They Do?** 何したの？

Student A stay on this page and **Student B** turn to **Appendix 4**. Tell your partner what the nine children did yesterday. Find six differences and circle those pictures.

Student A はこのページを見てください。Student B は Appendix 4 を見てください。9人の子供が昨日保育園で何を行ったかをパートナーに説明し，お互いの見ている絵に6つの違いを見つけて，その絵を丸で囲みましょう。

> **Example:** A: Yuki read a book.
> B: Yes, Yuki read a book. It's the same

Student A

* blocks 積み木

Practice 9

▶ **Pair Work**　ペアワーク

Look at the pictures below and take turns asking and answering questions. Use the example conversation as a model and the adjectives in the box.

下の絵を見てパートナーと順番に質問をし，答えてください。例文の会話を参考に，枠内の形容詞を使って文を作りましょう。

| naughty いたずらな | bored |
| grumpy 不機嫌な　helpful 役に立つ　~~sad~~ |
| sick　nervous　happy　sleepy　goofy |

Example: Ms. Markle:　How was Tina today?
　　　　　 Ms. Takahashi:　She was sad.

1. Alex

2. Seiji

3. Ken

4. Jasmine

5. Liam

6. Patrice

7. Somchai

8. Min-jun

9. Jock

Practice 10

▶ **Rewrite the Dialogue**　会話文を書きかえよう

Practice the dialogue below. Then work with a partner. Choose one picture below and rewrite the dialogue using the new words. After finishing, remember the dialogue and be ready to act it out.
以下の会話をパートナーと練習したあと，下の絵を見て元の会話を新しい語を使って書きかえましょう。書きかえた会話を暗記し，クラスメイトの前で発表してください。

> Father: How was Alan today?
> Ms. Sato: He seemed a little shy. He's new to our school, so I think it will change.
> Father: I hope so. He's usually not that way.
> Ms. Sato: We write in a message book* each day to keep you informed.* I'll let you know* if there are any problems.

* message book 連絡帳　　keep ~ informed ～に常に報告する　　let ~ know ～に知らせる

1. Sergei (he)
   was nervous /
   is not used to* school
   a note

2. Rina (she)
   seemed a little lonely* /
   is making friends
   an email

3. Wen (he)
   was a bit naughty /
   It was probably his cold
   a message

4. Olivia (she)
   seemed upset and cried /
   misses* her parents
   a text message*

5. Ibrahim (he)
   wouldn't go outside /
   It was cold today
   a note

6. Tanya (she)
   seemed quiet /
   This was her first day at school
   in a message book

* be used to ~ ～に慣れている　　lonely さびしい　　miss 恋しがる　　a text message 携帯のメール

Unit 14
Injuries and emergencies*
ケガと緊急事態

Speaking スピーキング

Dialogue 1

Mr. Hanson: What happened?
Kenny: I fell down* during recess. It hurts.
Mr. Hanson: That's too bad. Where does it hurt?
Kenny: Here. My arm.

Dialogue 2

Ms. Yamashita: What happened to your knee, Mari?
Mari: I fell down and scraped* it.
Ms. Yamashita: Oh no! How did that happen?
Mari: I was running with my brother on the way to my grandma's* house.
Ms. Yamashita: When did it happen?
Mari: Yesterday. But, I didn't tell anyone about it.
Ms. Yamashita: How come?
Mari: I thought I might get scolded.*

Dialogue 3

Ms. Ota: How did you hurt your head?
Tiffany: I fell off* the slide. It hurts.
Ms. Ota: You have a cut.* We'll go to the nurse's office and get a Band-Aid.*
Tiffany: OK. Is it bleeding?*
Ms. Ota: Just a little. You'll be fine.

* emergencies 緊急事態　　fall down ころぶ，倒れる　　scrape すりむく　　grandma (grandmother) 祖母
　　scold しかる　　fall off 落ちる　　cut 切り傷　　Band-Aid バンドエイド　　bleed 出血する

Unit 14 Injuries and emergencies

Key Words 86

Parts of the Body 体の部位

ankle 足首, くるぶし　　arm 腕　　back 背(中)　　bottom/buttocks 尻　　calf ふくらはぎ
cheek 頬　　chest 胸　　chin 顎　　ear 耳　　elbow 肘　　eye 眼　　eyebrow 眉毛
finger 指　　foot 足　　forehead 額　　hand 手　　head 頭, 頭部　　heel かかと
knee 膝　　leg 脚　　lip 唇　　mouth 口　　navel/belly button へそ　　neck 首
nose 鼻　　shoulder 肩　　stomach/abdomen 腹部　　thigh 腿, 大腿部　　thumb 親指
toe つま先　　tongue 舌　　tooth/teeth 歯　　waist 胴のくびれ, ウエスト　　wrist 手首

Look at the words for the parts of the body below and try to remember them.
下の絵を見て，体の部分を英語で覚えましょう。

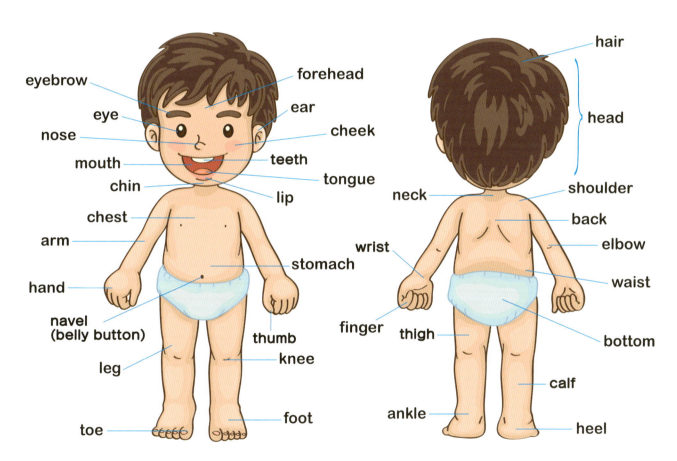

Practice 1

▶ **How Much Do You Remember?**　どのくらい覚えてる？

Work in pairs. How many words can you remember? Turn to **Appendix 5** and label the parts of the body.
体の部分をどのくらい覚えましたか？ パートナーといっしょに Appendix 5 を開いて体の部分を英語で書き入れましょう。

Practice 2

▶ Questions About the Body 体のどの部分？

Pair work: Use words from "Parts of the Body" to answer the following questions.
ペアワーク：質問の答えは体のある部分です。どの部分か答えましょう。

> **Example:** Question: We taste with this part of the body.
> Answer: <u>The tongue</u>.

1. What do boys have on top of their head that some men don't have? _____.
2. What part of the body opens and closes when you eat? _____.
3. What is in the middle of your leg? _____.
4. What is the part of the body between your head and your shoulders? _____.
5. What part of the body do we use to smell? _____.
6. Your hands have ten _____. Your feet have ten _____.
7. Name three things on your face? A _____, _____, and _____.
8. Your heart is inside your _____.
9. Your shortest and fattest finger is your _____.

Practice 3

▶ Parts of the Body Bingo ビンゴゲーム

Choose 12 words from the box and write them on the bingo card. Then listen to your teacher describe different body parts. Cross off the words corresponding to the hints. When you have crossed off four words in a row on your card, shout "Bingo!"

枠内から12の単語を選び，ビンゴカードに書いてください。先生が説明する体の部分に相当する単語を消していき，消したものが縦，横，斜めのいずれかで4つ繋がったら「ビンゴ！」と言ってください。

leg	lip	thumb	toe	ear	eye	knee
hand	waist	mouth	chest	back	nose	
head	shoulder	ankle	wrist	foot		

Unit 14 Injuries and emergencies

Bingo Card

Key Words 87

Injuries
break a bone (broken bone) 骨折する（骨折）　　bruise 青あざ　　swell (swollen) 腫れる（腫れた）
cut 切り傷　　bump こぶ　　burn ヤケド　　sprain 捻挫（する）　　scrape すりむく　　hurt 痛む, 痛める

Grammar
Past Tense 2
過去形2

88

Question	Answer
When did you hurt your leg?	I hurt it yesterday.
How did you break your arm?	I was in a car accident.*
When did the pain begin?	It began this morning.
Where did you hit your head?	I hit it here. I have a bump.

* accident 事故, おもらし

111

Practice 4

▶**Verbs** 動詞

Change the verbs in the sentences below. カッコ内の動詞を適切な形にかえましょう。

Nurse: How _____ (do) you get these cuts and scrapes* on your face?

Patient: I fell down.

Nurse: When _____ (do) it happen?

Patient: It _____ (happen) about 30 minutes ago.

Nurse: _____ (do) you get hurt anywhere else?*

Patient: Yes. I _____ (fall) on my left arm and it really hurts. Maybe I _____ (break) it.

Nurse: Yes, I can see you _____ (injure) it.

* scrape すり傷　　else ほかに

Practice 5

▶**Word Practice** 事故やケガに関する単語

Put the correct words from the box in the sentences below. Use each word once. Change the verbs to the correct tense when necessary.

枠内から適切な単語を一回だけ選び，正しい形にして空欄に入れましょう。

verbs

cut　bleed　fall　break　sprain　bump　burn　~~bruise~~*　hurt　feel

nouns

bump こぶ　　blister 水ぶくれ

Example:
I <u>bruised</u> my knee.

1. Oh, no! You _____ your leg.

* bruise 青あざをつくる

112

2. I _____ down and hit my head.

   Now, I _____ dizzy.

3. I _____ my ankle when playing soccer.

   It _____ when I walk.

4. He _____ his hand with a knife and

   it's _____ .

5. I _____ my finger when I touched a hot pan.

   Now, I have a _____ .

6. The boy _____ his head on the jungle gym and

   has a _____ on his head.

Practice 6

▶ **Listening** リスニング

Listen and write in the missing words in the notes from the parent (Ms. Wilson) and the teacher (Takeda Sensei).

保護者 (Ms. Wilson) と先生 (Takeda Sensei) のメッセージを聞いて，空欄を埋めましょう。

Dear Takeda Sensei,

Tina _____ for two days because she had a cold and _____ . She _____ , so I'm sending her to* school today. However, she might still _____ _____ . Please call me if there _____ .

　　　　　　　　　　　　　　　　　　　　　　　　　　　　Yours, Janet Wilson

Dear Ms. Wilson,

Tina was OK _____ but she had a stomachache once _____ and she _____ twice. She had diarrhea _____ . She ate normally* and _____ _____ in the afternoon, so I think _____ .

　　　　　　　　　　　　　　　　　　　　　　　　　　Sincerely, Namiko Takeda

---

* send (someone) to 〜に送る 　　normally 通常は

Practice 7

▶ **Complete the Story** 話を完成させよう

Complete the story about Kamal's accident. Use the words in the box. Change the verbs to the past tense.

枠内の単語を使い，カマルの事故についての説明を完成させましょう。動詞は過去形にしてください。

Unit 14 Injuries and emergencies

verbs

go   walk   tell   stay   fall down   have

nouns

doctor   crutches 松葉づえ   broken leg   hospital   stairs 階段   ambulance 救急車

Kamal's Accident

Kamal _____ an accident. He _____ _____

some _____ . He _____ to the _____ by

_____ . The _____ _____ him that he had a

_____ _____ . He _____ in the hospital for two

weeks. After that, he still had to _____ with _____ .

Practice 8

▶ **Role Play**   ロールプレイ

Make a conversation between a student and a teacher. Imagine the student had an accident. Use your imagination!
先生と生徒の会話を作り、お互いに練習してみましょう。生徒が事故にあったという想定です。想像力を発揮させてください！

Teacher: What happened?

Student: I _____.

Teacher: Oh no! How did that happen?

Student: I _____.

Teacher: When did it happen?

Student: _____.

Teacher: Does it hurt?

Student: _____.

Practice 9

▶ **Message Book**   連絡帳

Imagine that one of your students became sick, injured, or upset at kindergarten. Write a note to the parents. Imagine a name and then write about what happened.
幼稚園で生徒が病気になったり、ケガをしたり、動揺したことを保護者に伝えることになったとします。まず生徒の名前を決め、何が起こったのかを説明するメッセージを書きましょう。

Note from Stanton International Kindergarten

Name of child: _____

Date: _____

Problem:

_____

_____

_____

_____

Unit 15

We're going to go outside

外で遊ぼう

Speaking　スピーキング

Dialogue 1
 90

Ms. Suzuki: We're going to play outside now. First, change your shoes.
Lisa: OK. Hey, don't bump* me, Ryan!
Ms. Suzuki: Wait your turn, Ryan. OK everyone, let's make a line.

Dialogue 2
91

Mr. Takahashi: We're going to play in the sandbox now.
Riku: Yay! I'll get my sandbox set.
Mr. Takahashi: I see your bucket but where's your shovel?
Riku: I don't know. I'll go look for it.

Dialogue 3
 92

Rio: I'm going to play outside!
Ms. Imura: Don't run, Rio! Do you remember? No running in the hallway.
Rio: OK.
Ms. Imura: What are you going to do outside?
Rio: Play tag. Who wants to play tag?
Yuna: I do!
Miyu: I do too!
Rio: OK, who's going to be "it"?
Yuna: Me, me!
Miyu: Me first!

* bump　ぶつかる

Grammar 1
Future Tense 1
未来形 1

I'm (I am) going to call your name.　　I'll (I will) call your name.

We're (We are) going to take a nap now.　　We'll (We will) take a nap now.

We're (We are) not going to go outside today.　　We won't (We will not) go outside today.

Who's (Who is) going to pick you up?　　Who'll (Who will) pick you up?

Practice 1

▶**Listening** リスニング

Listen to the conversation and write in the missing words.　会話を聞いて空欄を埋めましょう。

Ms. Takeda: _____ , everyone! October 5th is Sports Day.

We're _____ many activities _____ .

What _____ to do? Anyone?

Tanya: We _____ !

Rika: We're going _____ !

Ms. Takeda: That's right. And your mom and dad _____

your performance.* Maybe your grandma and grandpa* _____ ,

_____ .

Jun: My brother _____ !

*performance 演技　　grandpa (grandfather) 祖父

Unit 15 We're going to go outside

95

Grammar 2
Future Tense 2
未来形 2

When you decide to do something suddenly without a prior plan, use "will" for the future. Otherwise, you can use either "will" or "be going to."

計画なく突然決めたことについて話すときは "will" を使います。このような場合以外は "will" か "be going to" どちらでも使えます。

A: I hurt my finger.　　　　　　　　　　　指をケガしちゃった。
B: Oh, I'll get you a Band-Aid.　　　　　　えー，バンドエイド取ってくるね。

A: It's raining today.　　　　　　　　　　今日雨だね。
B: In that case, we'll play inside.　　　　 じゃあ，家の中で遊ぼう。

When you are not sure about your future plan, use "will" for the future.
未来のことについて不確定なときは，"will" を使います。

A: What are you going to do?　　　　　　　何するの？
B: Maybe I'll read a book.　　　　　　　　たぶん本を読む。

Practice 2

▶ **Future Tense** 未来形

Use the verbs in parentheses in the future tense to complete the sentences. Use "going to" for all sentences except those that must use "will."

カッコ内の動詞を未来形にかえて文を完成させましょう。
"will" でなければならない文以外は "going to" を使いましょう。

1. I _____ (have) a birthday party on Friday.

2. After lunch, we _____ (go) outside and play.

3. Student: I spilled my milk!

   Teacher: I _____ (get) a towel to wipe it up.

4. For lunch today, we _____ (eat) curry rice.

5. I'm not sure which book to read. Maybe I _____ (read) this one.

6. A: Help me clean up.

   B: OK. I _____ (pick up) the toys.

Practice 3

▶Asking About Future Plans　今後の予定について聞こう

Take turns asking questions to each other. Write down your partner's answers.
パートナーと順番にお互いの予定を聞いて，書いてみましょう。

1. What are you going to do after your last class today?
   _____

2. What are you going to do this weekend?
   _____

3. What are you going to do after you graduate?*
   _____

4. What will you do on your next vacation?
   _____

* graduate 卒業する

Practice 4

▶Fill in the Blanks　穴埋め問題

The following sentences describe future events. Fill in the blanks using the words listed in the box.
以下は未来のことを表す文です。枠内の語を使って空欄を埋めましょう。

> help 手伝う　　introduce 紹介する　　call 呼ぶ
> pick ~ up ～を迎えに行く　　be on the stage ステージに上がる

1. Hi everyone, I _____ myself. My name is Hana.（will を使って）

2. Who _____ me clean the classroom?
   （be going to を使って）

3. OK, are you ready* to dance for all your parents? We _____
   _____ .（be going to を使って）

4. Teacher:　Ken, who _____ you _____
   today?（be going to を使って）

   Ken:　My grandmother. My mother is working today.

5. When you all sit down, I _____ your name.（will を使って）

* be ready 準備ができている

Grammar 3
Present Continuous Tense Used for the Future
現在進行形で未来を表す

96

We often use the present continuous tense instead of the future tenses ("be going to" and "will") to talk about the future.
"will" や "be going to" のほかに，現在進行形でも未来を表すことができます。

I'll leave soon. ➡ I'm leaving soon.
もうすぐ行くよ。（ここを出るよ）

Are you going to work today? ➡ Are you working today?
今日は（これから）仕事？

Practice 5

▶Talking about the Future with ~ing　現在進行形で未来を表す

Translate the following sentences using the present continuous tense to express the future tense, as in the example.
以下の未来を表す日本文を，例文を参考にして，現在進行形を使って英語にしてみましょう。

Example: 今日はこれから仕事なの。
I'm working today.（be 動詞 ＋ ~ing）

Translation

1. 外に行きますよ。（We ではじめる）　_____ .
2. ドアを閉めるわよ。　_____ .
3. 明日（ぼくたち）動物園に行くの？　_____ ?
4. ケンちゃんは今日学校に来ないのよ。　_____ .
5. 友達とランチを食べるの。　_____ .

Practice 6

▶Writing ライティング

Complete the following sentences using either the future tense or the present continuous tense. Use your imagination.

前の文に続く未来形の文を，自分で考えて作りましょう。will / be + going to / 現在進行形のうちどれを使ってもかまいません。

1. You have to get ready soon, because _____ .
2. My mom is sick, so my dad _____ .
3. It's a nice day out, so we _____ .
4. Tomorrow is Sports Day, so _____ .
5. Next Monday is my birthday _____ .

Practice 7

▶Find Someone Who こんな人いるかな？

Find someone who answers "yes" to each question and then write their names on the right. Ask an additional question using the question prompts on the left and write notes on the right. Talk to as many people as you can.

以下の表の左側の質問文を完成させてください。その質問に "Yes" と答えられる人を探し，その人の名前を右側の欄に記入してください。できるだけ多くの人に質問してみましょう。

Find someone who ...	Names + Extra Information
1. ... is studying tonight. Extra question: What ...?	
2. ... is shopping this weekend. Extra question: What ...? or Where ...?	
3. ... is having a birthday this month. Extra question: What date ...?	
4. ... is going on a trip during the next vacation. Extra question: Where ...?	
5. ... is eating at a restaurant tonight. Extra question: Where ...? or What ... eat?	
6. ... is playing a sport this weekend. Extra question: What ...?	
7. ... is watching TV tonight. Extra question: What ...?	
8. ... is meeting a friend after school. Extra question: Who ...?	

Review of Units 9 to 15
Unit 9 〜 15 までの復習

Practice 1   Listening   リスニング 97

Listen to the teacher talk about a student performance and write in the missing words.
先生が生徒の演技について話をしています。空欄を埋めましょう。

(On the stage)

Ms. Saito: We _____ show you a great performance today.

The children _____ for this day, so please give them a big hand!*

Audience:* (Applause*)

(The teacher talks to her students backstage.)

Ms. Saito: OK everyone, please gather here.* _____ to go on stage after the opening ceremony.* _____ Takeshi?

Kaito: He _____ .

Ms. Saito: Really? We _____ for the stage soon. I'm worried.

Kaito: He _____ .

Ms. Saito: Really? We _____ for the stage soon. I'm worried.

Kaito: Oh, _____ !

Ms. Saito: Phew!*

Mari: _____ to go on stage! Whoopee!*

Ms. Saito: Wow, Mari, _____ such a good mood!*

Yoko: I'm so nervous!

Ms. Saito: I can see that, but _____ . _____ just fine.

Yoko: OK, I'll try _____ .

Ms. Saito: Way to go* Yoko!

123

(After the performance)

Ms. Saito: You guys* did such an amazing job!* You _____
talented.* I'm so proud* _____!

Yoko: _____ .

Takeshi: Now I'm all sweaty. _____ this towel?

Ms. Saito: _____ .

Kaito: Do you think _____ first prize?*

Ms. Saito: Let's wait and see.*

> * give ~ a (big) hand 拍手する   audience 観客   applause 拍手   gather 集まる，集める
> opening ceremony 開会式   Phew! ふーっ！   Whoopee! やったー！   mood 気分
> Way to go! よくやったね！   guys あなたたち   amazing job! よくやったね！
> talented 才能がある   proud 誇りに思う   prize 賞   wait and see 様子を見る

Practice 2   Message to a Parent   保護者への連絡

Put the verbs into the correct tense in the spaces below.
カッコ内の動詞を適切な時制に直して空欄を埋めましょう。

Dear Mr. Morimoto,

Today, Makoto _____ (cry) a little after you left, but he _____ (stop) crying when he _____ (start) to _____ (play) with his friends. He _____ (be) very hungry. He _____ (love) the bread, but he _____ (leave) some spinach. Did he _____ (eat) breakfast this morning?

He _____ (do) not want to _____ (brush) his teeth after lunch, but he _____ (sleep) well during naptime. After the nap, we _____ (sing) songs. He _____ (be) very cheerful the rest of the day.

Practice 3   Feelings   気持ちを表す

In a group, share the feelings you have in the following situations.
以下の状況で，自分がどんな気持ちになるかをグループ内でシェアしてみましょう。

1. When I have a test, I feel _____ .
2. When I watch a baseball game, I feel _____ .
3. When I see a large dog walking toward me, I feel _____ .
4. When I'm in an airplane, I feel _____ .
5. When I arrive to school on Monday morning, I feel _____ .
6. When my friend gets a high score on a test, I feel _____ .

Practice 4   Arts and crafts   図画工作

Listen and practice the dialogue below.
以下の会話を聞いてパートナーと練習しましょう。

98

Ms. Saito: May fifth is a special holiday. Does anyone know what day it is?
Makoto: Children's Day!
Ms. Saito: Yes, it's Children's Day. What do we see on Children's Day?
Yuka: Carp streamers!*
Ms. Saito: That's right, Yuka. We're going to make carp streamers today. I'll give you some yarn,* colored paper,* glue, and a bottle of glitter.* I'll show* you how to make them. When we finish,* we'll display* them in the hallway. Your parents can see them when they visit.

* carp streamer 鯉のぼり   yarn 毛糸   colored paper 色紙   glitter（装飾用の）キラキラ光る細かい素材
show 見せる   finish 終わる，終える   display 見せる

Now, let's think of a project for children. Choose a holiday from the box. Write a dialogue like the dialogue above.
次の様々な祭日とそれに向けたプロジェクトを考えましょう。祝祭日を枠内から選び，上の会話を参考にして，先生と生徒になったつもりで会話を作ってみましょう。

> Mother's Day   New Year's Day   Christmas   Tanabata

Appendix 1

Take turns asking questions and write down the answers in the blanks below, as shown in the example.

パートナーと交代で質問をし，空欄に正しい国名，国籍，言語を入れましょう。

> **Example:** Student A: Where is Yelena from?
> Student B: She's from Russia.
> Student A: How do you spell "Russia"?
> Student B: "R-U-S-S-I-A." What's her nationality?*
> Student A: She's Russian. What language does she speak?
> Student B: She speaks Russian.

*nationality 国籍

Student B

	Name	Country	Nationality	Language
1.	Yelena (she)	Russia	Russian	Russian
2.	Charlotte (she)	United Kingdom	_____	English
3.	Min-jun (he)	Korea	Korean	_____
4.	Mai (she)	_____	_____	Vietnamese
5.	Somchai (he)	Thailand	_____	_____
6.	Adam (he)	_____	American	English
7.	Yun (she)	China	_____	Chinese
8.	Miguel (he)	_____	Brazilian	_____

Appendix 2

Tell your partner what the eight children are doing. Find six differences and circle those pictures.
8人の子供たちが何をしているかをパートナーに説明し，お互いの見ている絵に6つの違いを見つけて，その絵を丸で囲みましょう。

Example: A: Reiko is swinging on a swing.
B: Yes, Reiko is swinging on a swing. It's the same.

Student B

* jungle gym ジャングルジム　　monkey bars うんてい

Appendix 3

Work in pairs. Give hints to help your partner guess each word in your crossword below. When he/she guesses a word correctly, they should write it in their puzzle.

パートナーにクロスワードに入る単語をあてられるよう、英語でヒントをあげてください。わかったらその単語を書き入れましょう。

Example: A: What is 19 down?
B: It is the opposite of "now."
A: Is it "then"?
B: Yes, that's it!

Student B

Appendix 4

Tell your partner what the nine children did yesterday. Find six differences and circle those pictures.

9人の子供が昨日保育園で何を行ったかをパートナーに説明し、お互いの見ている絵に6つの違いを見つけて、その絵を丸で囲みましょう。

Example: A: Yuki read a book.
B: Yes, Yuki read a book. It's the same.

Student B

* stuffed animal ぬいぐるみ

Appendix 5

Parts of the Body

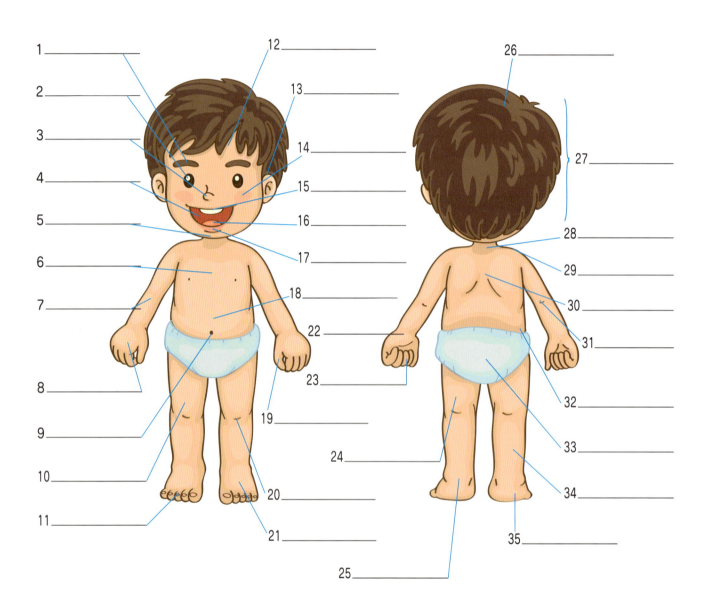

Glossary ＜用語集＞

A

abdomen	腹部	109
accident	事故, おもらし	111,115
achoo	くしゃみ [ハクション]	17
active	活動的な	46
afraid	怖がる	51,102
air conditioner (air-conditioned)	エアコン（エアコンの効いた）	87
amazing job!	よくやったね！	124
ambulance	救急車	30,115
ankle	足首, くるぶし	109,110,113
angry	怒っている	40,43
apologize	あやまる	90
appetite	食欲	19
applause	拍手	123
apron	エプロン	11
Are you kidding?	うそでしょ？	81
arrive	到着する	63,95,125
arm	腕	78,108,109,111,112
ashamed	恥じる	40,44
at least	少なくとも	23,24,73,94
audience	観客	41,123
aunt	おば	52

B

back	背（中）	109,110
backache	腰痛	27
backpack	リュックサック, バックパック	11,64
bandages	包帯	30
Band-Aid	バンドエイド	30,108,119
bang	ドアなどを強くたたく音 [ドン, バン]	17
bath towel	バスタオル	11
Be nice.	やさしくね。	55,57,77
be ready	準備ができている	120
be used to ~	～に慣れている	107
beep beep	車のクラクションの音 [ブー ブー]	17
belongings	持ち物	94
bend	曲げる, 曲がる	63,78
bib	よだれかけ	11
(a) bit	少し	38,72,107
bite (a bite)	かみつく（ひとくち）	58,73
blanket	毛布	11,94,95
bleed (blood)	出血する（血液）	108,112
blister	水ぶくれ	112
blocks	積み木	70,105
blow one's nose	～の鼻をかむ	59
boo hoo	人の泣き声 [ウェーンウェーン, シクシク, メソメソ]	17
boom	ドカーン	17
boring (bored)	つまらない（たいくつな）	39,40,41,44,51,79,106
borrow	借りる	78
bossy	いばった, いばっている	46,47,48
bottom	尻, おしり, すそ, 底	92,109
Boy!	わぁー！	104
brave	勇気がある	38,47
break a bone (broken bone)	骨折する（骨折）	111
brother	兄, 弟	39,41,46,52,53,108,118
brother-in-law	義理の兄（弟）	52
bruise	青あざ, 青あざをつくる	111,112
brush (one's teeth)	（～の歯を）磨く	20,23,24,95,96,98,124
bucket	バケツ	74,117
bully	いじめっこ, いじめる	38
bump	こぶ, ぶつかる	111,112,117
burn	ヤケド, 焼く, 焼ける	111,112
buttocks	尻	109
by himself/herself	彼／彼女 ひとりで	101

C

calf	ふくらはぎ	109
call	呼ぶ	6,13,114,118,120
Calm down.	落ち着きなさい。	77
careful	気をつける, 注意深い	57,58,77,79
carp streamer	鯉のぼり	125
carrot	ニンジン	68,73
cartoons	マンガ	20
cast	ギプス	30
cat's cradle	あやとり	76
cause	引き起こす（原因）	94
change into	着替える	33
change clothes	着替える	79
change of (clothes)	着替え	94
check-up (medical check-up)	健康診断	24
cheek	頬（ほお）	109
cheerful	明るい	46,47,124
chest	胸	109,110
chew	噛（か）む	68
childhood education	幼児教育	10
chin	顎（あご）	97,109
choke	のどを詰まらせる	68
chopsticks	お箸	11,70

chores	家事, 雑用	86
circle (make a circle)	円（円を作る）	57,58
clay	粘土	64,100
clean	清潔な	79
climb	登る	76
cock a doddle do	ニワトリの鳴き声［コケコッコー］	17
cold	風邪	26,27,28,107,114
color pencil	色えんぴつ	64
colored paper	色紙	125
come over	こっちに来る	57
complain	文句を言う	58,68,73,77
confusing (confused)	混乱する（混乱した）	39,40,41,44,51
cool down	冷める, 冷ます	72
cotton swabs	綿棒	30
cough (coughing)	咳（咳をする）	27,28,29,64
cough syrup	咳止めシロップ	30
cousin	いとこ	52,64
crash	壊れる音［ガシャン］	17
crayon	クレヨン	64
cross	横切る	56
crowded	混んでいる	12
crunch crunch	食べるときのカリカリ音	17
crutches	松葉づえ	30,115
cubby (cubbyhole)	小さな収納スペース	97
cut	切り傷（切る）	66,108,111,112
cut in line	列に割り込む	84
cut out	切り抜く	74

D

dangerous (danger)	危険な, 危ない（危険）	56,57,79,85
daughter	娘	52
decide	決める	103,119
degree	度	87
dentist	歯医者	27,28
difficult	難しい	72,79
dig	掘る	76
directions	指示	44
dirty	汚い, 汚れた	32,79,97
disappointing (disappointed)	がっかりする（がっかりした）	39,41,43,44
display	見せる	125
dive (diving)	飛び込む（飛び込み）	56,85
dizzy	めまいがする	28,29,64,113
don't be shy	恥ずかしがらないで	55,57
drawer	引き出し	74
drip	たれる	97
dry	乾かす, 乾いた	55,57,79
during	〜の間（期間）	54,108,122,124

E

ear	耳	109,110
early	早い	18,79,85,86
easy	簡単な	44,79
elbow	肘（ひじ）	109
elderly	高齢者	48
else	ほかに	112
embarrassing (embarrassed)	恥ずかしい, 恥ずかしがる	39,40
emergency (emergencies)	緊急（の）（緊急事態）	108
empty	空の	79
entrance	入口, 玄関	56
eraser	消しゴム	64
exciting (excited)	わくわくする	13,39,40,41,44,64,79,82
exercise	運動（する）	24
extra	追加の, 予備の	85,94,97,122
eye	目	33,109,110
eyebrow	眉毛（まゆげ）	109
eye drops	目薬	30

F

face ~	〜のほうに向く	63
fall down	ころぶ, 倒れる	108,112,115
fall off	落ちる	108
far	遠い	12,79
father	父	18,52,107
faucet	蛇口	32
favorite	お気に入りの	68,102
feed	（動物などに）エサをやる	56
feel better	気分がよくなる	26
fever	熱	26,27,28,64,84
field trip	遠足	85,93
find out	（情報を）知る	72
find	見つける	45,78,96,97
finger	指	74,109,110,113,119
fingernail	手の指の爪	70
finish	終わる, 終える	43,74,79,103,125
fill-out	記入する	93
first in line	一番先	84
flip-flops	ビーチサンダル	94
fold	たたむ, 折る	66
follow	従う	60
following	以下の	94
foot	足, くるぶしから下の部分	109,110
forehead	額	31,109
foreign (foreigner)	外国の（外国人）	16
form	書式, 用紙	85,93,96
fried rice	チャーハン	73
front (in front)	前方の（前の）	40,63

frustrating (frustrated)	イライラする（している）, 欲求不満	38,39,40
full	（お腹などが）いっぱい	79

G

gargle	うがいをする	84
gather	集まる, 集める	123
generous	気前がよい, 寛大な	47,48
get along (with)	仲良くする	9,90
get dressed	着替える	33
get off	降りる	55,78
get on	乗る	76,78
get ready	準備する	33,70,96,122
give ~ a hand	拍手する, ~を手伝う	123
glitter	（装飾用の）キラキラ光る細かい素材	125
glue	のり	64,125
go back	戻る	32,70
go outside	外に行く	55,57,63,68,69,74,85,107,117,118,119
good job	よくやったね	100,101
goofy	ふざけた, お茶目な	46,47,48,64,106
graduate	卒業する	120
granddaughter	孫娘	52
grandfather (grandpa)	祖父	52,64,81,118
grandmother (grandma)	祖母	52,108,118,120
grandson	孫息子	52
grump (grumpy)	文句ばかり言う人（不機嫌な）	106
guess	あてる	97
guys	あなたたち	101,124

H

hallway	ろうか	56,57,63,117,125
hand	手	21,32,55,60,63,70,73,84,85,93,95,109,110,113,123
hang	掛ける	54
hang out	出かける, 出歩く	8,9,75
hang up	電話を切る	54
happen	起こる	108,112,116
hard	一生懸命に	44
have a sip	一口すする	72
head	頭, 頭部	31,80,108,109,110,111,113
headache	頭痛	26,27,28
health insurance card	保険証	30
heel	かかと	109
helpful	役に立つ	106
Here they are.	あっ, あった。	74
hide-and-seek	かくれんぼ	15,71,76,77
highlighter	蛍光ペン	64
Hold on.	ちょっと待って。	77
homework	宿題	20,23,41,72,79,86,103
honest	正直な	47,48,64
honk honk	車のクラクションの音［プー プー］	17
hopscotch	けんけんぱ	76
How nice!	なんてすてき！	102
huge	巨大な	97
hurry (be in a hurry)	急ぐ（急いでいる）	51
hurry up	急ぐ	33,77,78,84
hurt	痛む, 痛める	26,29,81,85,108,111,112,116,119
husband	夫	52

I

I bet ~	それは~に違いない	12
ice pack	アイスパック	30
I knew it!	やっぱり！ 思った通り！	102
in that case	その場合	84,119
indoor shoes	上履き	11,56,85
influenza (the flu)	インフルエンザ	27,29
inform	知らせる	107
injury	ケガ	94
interesting (interested)	おもしろい（興味がある）	39,43
introduce	紹介する	57,120
irritating (irritated)	イライラする（イライラして）	41
itchy	かゆい	27,28,29

J

jealous	うらやましがる	40,44
join	参加する	77
jump rope	なわとび（をする）	34,76
jungle gym	ジャングルジム	36,113,127

K

keep ~ informed	~に常に報告する	107
kick-the-can	缶けり	76
kind	種類, 優しい	46,47,48,53
kindergarten	幼稚園	6,8,9,13,16,116
knee	膝（ひざ）	108,109,110,112

L

label	名前をつける	94
lap	ひざ（腰から膝頭までの水平な部分）	55
late	遅い	18,20,45,71,79
laugh	笑う, 笑い	46,48,55
laundry machine	洗濯機	97
laundry	洗濯	97
leave	置いたままにする, 置き忘れる, 残す, 出る, 出発する	57,95,121,124
leg	脚	109,110,111,112,115
lend	貸す	78

let ~ know	～に知らせる	107
lie (lying)	うそをつく（ついている）	38,44
line up	並ぶ	56
lip	唇	109,110
lonely	さびしい	107
look forward to ~	～を楽しみにする	6
loose	ゆるい	79
lose	負ける, なくす	45,78
lunchbox	お弁当箱	11

M

make a line	列をつくる	84,117
make a circle	円をつくる	57,58
make mistakes	間違う	102
make sure	必ず～する	93,94,95
math (mathematics)	算数	14,41,44,79,81
mean	いじわるな	38
medicine	薬	26
mental (mentally)	精神の（精神的に）	9
meow	ネコの鳴き声［ニャー］	17
mess (messy)	ゴチャゴチャした, 面倒な（状況） 49,51,57,58,73	
mess up	ゴチャゴチャにする	49
message book	連絡帳	95,107,116
miss	恋しがる	12,107
monkey bars	うんてい	36,76,127
moo	牛の鳴き声［モー］	17
mood	気分	123
mother	母	14,18,26,44,48,49,52,81,97,104,120
mother-in-law	義理の母	52
mouth	口	97,109,110
move over	ずれる	55
musical instruments	楽器	63

N

nap	昼寝（をする）	33,68,85,96,98,118,124
naptime	お昼寝の時間	33,54,85,94,95,124
napkin	ナプキン	68,97
nationality	国籍	14,126
naughty	いたずらな	47,48,106,107
navel (belly button)	へそ	109
near	近い	56,79
neck	首	109
need	必要な, 必要とする	28,33,71,77,84,85,92,94,95,103
nephew	甥	52
nervous	緊張した	43,64,106,107,123
niece	姪	52,64
noise	騒音	54
noisy	うるさい	68,79
normally	通常は	33,114
nose	鼻	58,109,110
nosebleed	鼻血	27
No way!	うそー！	81
nurse	看護師	30,108,112
nursery school	保育園	8,9

O

oink oink	ブタの鳴き声［ブーブー］	17
ointment	塗り薬	30
opening ceremony	開会式	123
Ouch (Ow)!	痛い！	74,81

P

pain	痛み	27,111
paint	絵の具, 絵を描く	45,57,64,81,100,101
paintbrush	絵筆	64,104
paper clips	ペーパークリップ	64
paper towel	キッチンペーパー, ペーパータオル	32
parts of the body	体の部分	109,130
pass	合格する	44,104
patient	患者, 我慢強い	30,38,77,112
pee	おしっこ	92
pencil sharpener	えんぴつ削り	64
performance	演技	118,123
permission slip	許可書	85
permission	許可	85
personality	性格	64
Phew!	ふーっ！	123
physical (physically)	身体の（身体的に）	9
pick up	迎えに行く／来る, ひろう	18,54,78,118,119,120
picky	好き嫌いがある	47,48,58,64,70
piece	一かけ, 一切れ	68
pile	山積み	97
pills	薬	30
pillow	まくら	11,94,95
play catch	キャッチボールをする	15,35,76
playground	園庭, 校庭	15,57,64,76,85
plenty (of)	たくさんの, 十分な	87
poo	うんち	92
pop	風船などが割れる音［パーン］	17
poor	まずしい	48
potty (go potty)	トイレ（トイレに行く）	59,92,95
practice	練習（する）	71,98
prefecture	県	7
prepare	準備をする	22,94
pretend	ふりをする	69
priority seat	優先席	48
prize	賞	124

Glossary

proud	誇りに思う	40,44,124
puddle	水たまり	58
pull down	（引き）降ろす	78
pull up	持ち上げる	78
pull	引く	78
purple	むらさき色（の）	102
push	押す	55,78,84,85,90
put ~ back	～を元（の位置）に戻す	74
put away	片づける	57
put on	着る, 身につける	63,66,78

Q

quiet	静かな	33,54,55,61,63,79,107

R

rain boots	長靴	11
raise (one's hands)	（手を）挙げる	60
rash	湿疹	27
recess	休み時間	57,78,108
recital	発表会	102
relaxed	リラックスした	39,40
relieved	安心した	40,46,51
restroom	トイレ	56,72,95
right	正しい	18,57,79,84,92,96,102,118,125
ring ring	電話の音［リンリン］	17
rip	破れる音［ピリッ］	17
roll up	まくる	72
rough	粗い, ざらざらした	79
rude	失礼な	47,48
ruff ruff	犬の鳴き声［ワンワン］	17
ruler	ものさし	64
run around	駆け回る	54,57
run away	逃げる	57
runny nose	鼻水の出ている鼻	58

S

safe	安全な	79
sandbox	砂場	35,64,74,75,76,117
sandcastle	砂のお城	49,69
scale	体重計	30
scared (be scared of ~)	怖がる（～が怖い）	38,41,45
scary	怖い	41,83,99
scissors	ハサミ	64,74
scold	しかる	108
Scotch tape	セロテープ	64
scrape	すりむく, すり傷	108,111,112
scream	叫ぶ	77,79
seesaw	シーソー	76
selfish	わがままな	68
send (someone) to ~	～に送る	114
serious	まじめな	46
serve	食事や飲み物を出す	37
set the table	テーブルに食事の用意をする（食器をテーブルにセットする）	70
sheet	シーツ	11
shocked	ショックな	39,40,42,44,64
shoelaces	靴ひも	101
shot	注射	30,81
shoulder	肩	109,110
shovel	シャベル	74,117
show	見せる	22,92,95,123,125
show respect	敬意を払う	9
shy	恥ずかしがりや	46,107
silly	バカな, ふざけた	46,47,48
sink	シンク, 流し	32
sip (a sip)	ひとくちすする（ひとすすり）	72,97
sister	姉, 妹	52
skit	スキット, 寸劇, 短い演劇	25,31
skin	肌	27
sleeve	袖	72
slide	すべり台	34,35,55,64,76,77,85,108
slow down (Slow down.)	ゆっくりさせる（あわてないで。）	77,78
smart	賢い	7,44,46,47
smooth	なめらかな	79
snap	棒などが折れる音［ポキン, パキン］	17
sneeze (sneezing)	くしゃみ（をする）	27
social skills	社会的な技能	9
someday	いつか	12
son	息子	28,46,52
sore throat	のどの痛み	27
sound(s) ~	～に聞こえる, ～だね, ～に思われる	15,18
spill	こぼす, こぼれる	57,70,79,81,119
spinach	ホウレンソウ	70,124
splash	水がはねる音［ピシャッ］	17
sprain	捻挫（する）	111,112
squeak squeak	ネズミの鳴き声［チューチュー］	17
stairs	階段	115
stapler	ホチキス	64
steal	盗む	48
sticker	シール	64
still	まだ	20,32,57,72,114,115
stink (stinky)	臭いにおいがする（臭い）	51,85
stomach (abdomen)	腹部	26,109
stomachache	腹痛, 胃痛	19,26,27,28,85,114
stop fighting	ケンカをやめる	55,57,58
stretch	伸ばす	78
stuffed animal	ぬいぐるみ	129

English	Japanese	Pages
superhero	スーパーヒーロー	69
sweat (sweaty)	汗（汗まみれの）	27,103,124
sweet	優しい	46,47
swell (swollen)	腫れる（腫れた）	111
swim cap	水泳帽	11
swimsuit	水着	11,95
swing	ブランコ	34,55,64,74,75,76,77,127
symptom	症状	27,64

T

tag	鬼ごっこ	15,69,76,117
take a bath/shower	お風呂に入る、シャワーをあびる	23
take a look	見る	72,100
take a rest	休む	72
take a shower	シャワーをあびる	23,24,58,103
take care	世話をする	26
Take it easy.	落ち着いてよ。じゃあね。	77
take off	脱ぐ	61,78,97
take turns	順番でする、交代でする	57,71,77,88
talented	才能がある	47,48,124
tambourine	タンバリン	71
taste	味がする、味わう	26,110
terrible	ひどい	81
terrific	すばらしい	15
(a) text message	携帯のメール	107
That's amazing!	すごい！	81
thermometer	体温計	30
Thermos	水筒	11,64
thigh	腿（もも）、大腿（だいたい）部	109
think about	について考える	72
throw away	捨てる	59,68
throw	投げる	58
thud	重いものが落ちる音［ドスン］	17
thumb	親指	109,110
tic-tac-toe	まるばつ	76
ticket window	切符売り場	56
tight	（服などが）きつい、しっかりと	79
tissues	ティッシュ	11,59
toe	つま先	109,110
toilet training (toilet-trained)	オムツの練習（オムツがとれた）	94
tongue	舌	109,110
tooth (teeth)	歯	109
toothache	歯痛	27,28,29
toothbrush	歯ブラシ	11,64,96,98
toothpaste	歯磨き粉	11,98
touch	さわる	55,57,113
tough	かたい、丈夫な	68
train platform	駅のホーム	56
trip	つまずく	55
truth	真実	44,48
tunnel	トンネル	76
turn away	（顔を）そむける	63
turn off	スイッチを切る、蛇口などを閉める	32,78
turn on	スイッチを入れる、蛇口などを開ける	78
turn	番	55,84,117
tweet tweet	鳥の鳴き声［ピーピー］	17
tweezers	ピンセット	30

U

uncle	おじ	52
underpants	下着のパンツ	11
underwear	下着	85,94,97
until ~	～まで	20,26,57,86
upset	怒っている	38,51,107

V

vegetable	野菜	85,86
vomit (vomiting)	吐く	27

W

waist	胴のくびれ、ウエスト	109,110
wait	待つ	20,68,77,79,84,85,92
wait and see	様子を見る	124
wait for (one's) turn	（人の）番を待つ	55,84,117
wallet	さいふ	45
wastebasket	ゴミ箱	68
Way to go!	よくやったね！	123
weather	天気	87
well done	よくできたね	100,101
wet	濡れた	57,79,85,97
what happened	何が起こったのか	72,108,116
What's the matter?	どうしたの？	18,31
What's wrong?	どうしたの？	74
wheelchair	車いす	30
whine	ぐずぐず言う	58
Whoa!	うわっ！	80
Whoopee!	やったー！	123
wife	妻	52
win	勝つ	78
wipe	拭く	32,58,92,97,119
would	（～だったら）～だろう	45
Wow!	ワーッ！	19,20,80,81,100,101,123
wrist	手首	109,110
wrong	間違った	44,79

Y

English	Japanese	Pages
yummy	おいしい	68

yarn	毛糸	125
Yay!	イェイ！	51,71,117
yell	叫ぶ	58
You did it!	やったね！	102
You sure can.	もちろん（やって）いいよ。	74
Yuck!	ゲーッ！	26,70,73,81

著作権法上、無断複写・複製は禁じられています。

Speaking of Childcare	[B-883]
保育学生のための英語コミュニケーション	

1　刷	2019年4月1日
5　刷	2024年3月29日
著　者	Peter Vincent　　ピーター ビンセント Naoko Nakazato　　中里　菜穂子
発行者 発行所	南雲　一範　　Kazunori Nagumo 株式会社　南雲堂 〒162-0801　東京都新宿区山吹町361 NAN'UN-DO Co., Ltd. 361 Yamabuki-cho, Shinjuku-ku, Tokyo 162-0801, Japan 振替口座：00160-0-46863 TEL:　03-3268-2311（営業部：学校関係） 　　　　03-3268-2384（営業部：書店関係） 　　　　03-3268-2387（編集部） FAX:　03-3269-2486
編集者	加藤　敦
組　版	柴崎　利恵
装　丁	銀　月　堂
イラスト	パント大吉
検　印	省　略
コード	ISBN978-4-523-17883-5　　C0082

Printed in Japan

E-mail : nanundo@post.email.ne.jp
URL : https://www.nanun-do.co.jp/